CITYSPOTS
RIGA

**Researched and updated by
Martins Zaprauskis**

Researched and updated by Martins Zaprauskis

Published by Thomas Cook Publishing
A division of Thomas Cook Tour Operations Limited
Company registration No: 1450464 England
The Thomas Cook Business Park, 9 Coningsby Road
Peterborough PE3 8SB, United Kingdom
Email: books@thomascook.com, Tel: +44 (0)1733 416477
www.thomascookpublishing.com

Produced by The Content Works Ltd
Aston Court, Kingsmead Business Park, Frederick Place
High Wycombe, Bucks HP11 1LA
www.thecontentworks.com

Series design based on an original concept by Studio 183 Limited

ISBN: 978-1-84157-875-0

First edition © 2006 Thomas Cook Publishing
This second edition © 2008 Thomas Cook Publishing
Text © Thomas Cook Publishing
Maps © Thomas Cook Publishing/PCGraphics (UK) Limited
Transport map © Communicarta Limited

Series Editor: Kelly Anne Pipes
Production/DTP: Steven Collins

Printed and bound in Spain by GraphyCems

Cover photography (Riflemen Monument and St Peters Church steeple)
© Peter Adams/Getty Images

CONTENTS

SYMBOLS KEY

The following symbols are used throughout this book:

ⓐ address ☎ telephone ⓕ fax Ⓦ website address
🕐 opening times Ⓝ public transport connections

The following symbols are used on the maps:

i	information office	▪	points of interest
✈	airport	◯	city
✚	hospital	◯	large town
🛡	police station	◦	small town
🚌	bus station	—	main road
🚊	railway station	—	minor road
✝	cathedral	—	railway
❶	numbers denote featured cafés & restaurants		

Hotels and restaurants are graded by approximate price as follows:
£ budget price **££** mid-range price **£££** expensive **£££+** most expensive

◗ *Old Rīga is dominated by spires*

INTRODUCING
Riga

Introduction

Riga engages in a delicate balancing act. One foot is firmly planted in the Soviet-influenced 20th century, while the other stands on tiptoe in the 21st.

With a population greater than 740,000, Riga is the Baltic States' largest city. It bustles with urban energy as it should, for commerce lies at its very heart. Once a member of the Hanseatic League, Riga owes its financial development to trade: this also gave the city its enchanting architecture. It is a treasure chest of design, from the sumptuousness of Nordic Gothic, Classic Symbolism, art nouveau and Constructivism, to the utilitarian influences of Soviet occupation. Riga's varied collection of architecture is so important that its historic centre, the Old Town, was added to the UNESCO World Heritage List in 1997.

Contributing to Riga's unusual nature is the ethnic split of the city. Just over half of its residents are Russian or Russian-speaking, the remainder being Latvian. The result is two communities appearing to lead completely separate lives: they read different newspapers, and listen to radio and television stations broadcast in their own language. Fortunately for the visitor, English is widely spoken.

Where the people of Riga join hands is in the celebration of sport. Hockey players, especially Latvian NHL stars, are revered as gods and each year thousands of fans, both Latvian and Russian, follow their national team to the World Championships. Some of the nation's best athletes are also ethnic Russians who have brought back gold and bronze medals from the Olympic Games and the coveted oak wreath from the New York Marathon. In short, whenever an athlete wears the maroon and white colours of the

Latvian flag, he or she is guaranteed to enjoy the support of all of Latvia's 2.3 million residents.

Riga is a little bit this and a little bit that. To some it has the cosy intimacy of Prague, the sophistication of Paris or the cosmopolitan flavour of Berlin. It has all that and more. It has its own personality, born of hardship, conquest and endurance. Whatever happens, Riga always emerges stronger than ever, having simply added one more layer to its soul; one more set of treasures for visitors to discover.

⬤ *Dome Square is taken over by the Christmas Market in December*

When to go

As Latvians are doomed to live in Northern Europe where winters are long and dark, they make the most of every warm, sunny day so it's best to go in summer. From June to August the beer gardens are full and the nearby beaches at Jūrmala are so crowded you can hardly see the sea. Music festivals and concerts are also part and parcel of a Latvian summer, so you're never short of something to do.

SEASONS & CLIMATE

In Riga, the weather is, with the exception of summer, almost invariably drizzly and cloudy. That said, the city has a very moderate, maritime climate, with summers that are not too hot, and winters not too cold. High summer humidity can make the city rather cloudy and damp, with over 700 mm (28 in) of precipitation a year on average. Although summer temperatures average 17°C (62°F), they can occasionally exceed 30°C (86°F).

ALL SINGING, ALL DANCING

The Latvian Song and Dance Festival has been celebrated ever since it was first held, in 1873. For one week every four years thousands of singers and dancers from all over Latvia gather for a festival of folk culture and life, held at various venues and culminating in a parade through the city to the grand open-air stage in Mežaparks. This festival boosts the self-esteem of Latvians, who originally created it as a response to the chauvinism of the local German and Russian elites. The next festival will take place in July 2008 (Ⓦ www.dziesmusvetki2008.lv).

Spring starts in mid-April, and comes in quickly. May, the first half of June, July, August and September are the best months to visit. Thundery showers are frequent during the last half of June. July, although the warmest month, is also the wettest, with frequent showers. March is the driest month.

Winter gets serious in November and lasts until March, with snow usually on the ground from mid-December until mid-March. Winter temperatures average -5°C (23°F) and rarely go over 4°C (39°F). Spring and autumn tend to be unpredictable, often with both sunshine and rain on the same day.

ANNUAL EVENTS

Latvia's major holidays can trace their roots to sun-worshipping pagan cultures. The most important is Līgo & Jāņi, or the Summer Solstice, celebrated on the nights of 23 and 24 June. This is when the city is emptied of people, as they head to the countryside to enjoy the shortest night of the year, which they spend in serious partying.

Christmas has always been a special event in Latvia, indeed in 1510 the world's first decorated Christmas tree was erected in Riga. Today, Riga's Christmas Market is one of the best in Europe.

February

International Bach Chamber Music Festival Concerts of Bach's chamber music pieces are held in buildings entirely appropriate to the music, as well as in larger concert halls. The festival also features master classes by famous musicians. Ⓦ www.music.lv/bachfestival

April

Baltic Ballet Festival Created in 1993, the Ballet Festival brings together ballet soloists, companies and choreographers from all three Baltic States. Ⓦ www.ballet-festival.lv

May
Riga International Marathon Annual event that draws runners from around the globe. Ⓦ www.marathon.lv

June
Early Music Festival Medieval music performed at a wide variety of venues, including some of Riga's most impressive Gothic churches.
Gadatirgus A massive arts and crafts festival held on the first weekend in June at the Open-Air Ethnographic Museum.
Līgo & Jāņi 23–4 June The annual midsummer pagan celebration. It's the best time to drink beer and celebrate the long summer days, and you can begin early at the Midsummer Market on 22 June on Dome Square.
Riga Opera Festival Over a period of 10 days, local and international opera stars perform at the Latvia National Opera. Ⓦ www.opera.lv

July
Baltic Beach Party Every July the city of Liepāja on the western coast of Latvia builds a stage on the beach and invites pop and techno stars perform to thousands of people. Ⓦ www.beachparty.lv
Organ Music Festival Europe's best organists tickle the ivories at Dome Cathedral.
Riga's Rhythms International Jazz Festival Jazz stars from around the globe flock to Riga each July for concerts at various venues throughout the Latvian capital. Ⓦ www.rigasritmi.lv
Saulkrasti Jazz Festival International jazz stars perform at this little-known festival, held each July at the seaside resort of Saulkrasti 30km north of Riga. Ⓦ www.saulkrastijazz.lv

August
Sacred Music Festival Riga choirs, composers and artists celebrate

the music of composers such as Bach, Berlioz and Beethoven at
churches and other venues. Ⓦ www.choirlatvija.lv

September
International Organ Music Festival, Liepāja Original organ compositions,
choirs and guest artists grace this festival held in Liepāja's famous
Church of the Holy Trinity. Ⓦ www.liepaja.lv

October
Arena New Music Festival For nearly the entire month, cutting-edge
experimental musicians from varied genres perform at venues in Riga.
Ⓦ www.arenafest.lv

December
Christmas Market Dozens of stalls selling anything from mulled
wine and gingerbread cookies to handmade sweaters and mittens
with Latvian designs cover Dome Square for the entire month.

PUBLIC HOLIDAYS
New Year's Day 1 Jan
Good Friday 21 March 2008, 10 April 2009
Easter Sunday 23 March 2008, 12 April 2009
Easter Monday 24 March 2008, 13 April 2009
Labour Day 1 May
Independence Day in 1990 4 May
Summer solstice celebrations (Līgo & Jāņi) 23–4 June
Independence Day in 1918 18 Nov
Christmas 24–6 Dec
New Year's Eve 31 Dec

Riga's Soviet legacy

Many of Riga's visitors are disappointed to discover that the city is like many other Western European capitals, with cobblestone streets, beautiful architecture and medieval churches. Where, they ask, are the remnants of 50 years of Soviet occupation? They want something ugly and exotic. They want Minsk.

Nearly all of the Communist-style edifices built in the city centre and Old Riga have been destroyed and replaced with either modern glass-and-steel structures or a re-creation of a centuries-old building destroyed during the war. And what became of Lenin? The statue of the Father of the Revolution that once stood in the middle of Brīvības bulvāris (Freedom Boulevard) was one of the first monuments to be knocked down after Independence.

Fortunately, for anyone who is willing to take a short trip via public transport, there are still some interesting symbols of that bygone era to be seen. You just have to know where to look. Take a tram across the Akmens Bridge to the Soviet Victory Monument, which boasts giant soldiers, Mother Russia and gold stars. Just beyond the Central Market you'll find the Academy of Sciences, the unsuccessful copy of the Empire State Building that was erected in large cities throughout the communist world. Hammers and sickles adorn the façade, and for a small fee you can take the lift to the observation platform on the 17th floor. A gold-painted frieze of a Red Army soldier carrying the flag of the USSR can be seen at the Pokrov Cemetery near Senču iela (take tram 11 to the Mēness iela stop). Finally, before you leave Riga you can also have a look at Soviet aircraft at the Riga Aviation Museum to the right of the main airport terminal.

◗ *Soviet Victory Monument in Pārdaugava*

History

Riga was founded in 1201 by German crusaders who brought
Christianity to local tribes at the point of a sword. Its location at
the mouth of the mighty River Daugava made it an ideal base for
traders eager to get their hands on amber, furs and timber, and by
1282 the town had joined the Hanseatic League, Europe's first trade
organisation. As a result of the Livonian War, Riga fell under the rule
of Poland in 1558, but obtained status as a free town in 1561. Then
Poland waged war with Sweden, and in 1621 Riga fell to the Swedes.
Sweden, in turn, lost the city to the Russians. In 1812, the city's
wooden suburbs were razed in expectation of a Napoleonic army
that never arrived. After this, the street plan that still exists today
was created.

Under the tsars, Riga thrived. Industry rapidly grew, and the city
became one of the main seaports of the Russian Empire, expanding
until it was second only to St Petersburg in western Russia. It was
during this period that most of its art nouveau architecture
(*Jugendstil*) was built.

World War I was devastating to Riga. At the outbreak of war, the
city was on the front line, and about 200,000 of its inhabitants fled,
while its numerous industrial enterprises were evacuated to Central
Russia. On 18 November 1918, with the collapse of Germany and
with Russia weak from revolution, Latvia proclaimed independence.
However, it took another two years of prolonged fighting to establish
that status. In August 1920, a peace treaty with Russia was signed
and Riga became the capital of a free Latvia. Once again it became
a robust seaport, with development of industry as well as culture
and education. Independence lasted only 20 years, until World War II.
On 17 June 1940, Russian tanks rolled onto the streets of Riga; the

following year the Germans threw the Russians out of the city; two years later, the Russians were back. The city and its inhabitants suffered greatly.

Under Soviet occupation, Riga once again became an industrial juggernaut, and hundreds of thousands of Russians were sent to Riga to man its factories. These jobs weren't offered to local Latvians in an attempt to dilute the nation's ethnic composition, which is why Riga now has a high proportion of ethnic Russians.

Latvians were among the first people in the USSR to embrace glasnost and perestroika in the 1980s, which led to the independence movement. A declaration to restore independence was adopted on 4 May 1990. The Kremlin was not amused. In January 1991 the population of Latvia gathered on barricades to face the Russian military. Finally, on 21 August 1991, Latvia once more declared independence. On 1 May 2004 Latvia joined the EU, in effect rejoining the symbolic community to which it once belonged. Latvians now have a chance to tackle domestic issues such as poverty and corruption. The country's popular president Vaira Vīķe-Freiberga was replaced by orthopaedic surgeon Valdis Zatlers in July 2007. The renowned doctor has admitted to accepting gifts and not reporting them as income. Only time will tell if he can fill the enormous shoes of his predecessor.

🔺 *The flag of independent Latvia*

Lifestyle

Which Riga will you visit? The traditional city, with its medieval architecture, folk singing and hearty food, or the new Riga of expensive luxury cars, raging nightlife and bohemian wireless internet cafés?

An economic boom spurred by EU membership, international banks with loose lending policies and a soaring property market has brought unprecedented wealth to the shrewd and just plain lucky of Riga. The drabness and peeling paint of the Soviet era has been replaced by colourful, completely renovated buildings that look better now than they did 100 (or even 400) years ago when they were new. A decaying infrastructure has given way to state-of-the-art technology, and your average Rigan wouldn't be caught in a naff furry hat with last year's Nokia mobile phone or, God forbid, an outdated 1GB iPod. In fact, the new generation of Latvians, especially the ones who can hardly remember the breadlines of the past, pay their bills on-line and get their weather reports and news via text messages.

The bistros and boozers of the past have also gone the way of the USSR. Rigans now e-mail friends from their notebooks while sipping cappuccinos at trendy coffee shops or while away an evening drinking chocolate martinis at hip cocktail bars that would hold their own in London or New York. Naturally, only the latest fashions will do. Unfortunately, all of this conspicuous consumption comes at an increasing cost. Although wages are slowly rising, the prices of goods and services have skyrocketed. Anything imported will cost you much more than you would pay in Western Europe, and even that most sacred of local Latvian products, beer, can cost as much as 3Ls a pint at an upmarket bar or restaurant. The rising cost of living and runaway inflation has many Latvians pining for the good old days – those being post-communism and pre-EU.

Although some of the younger generation gladly worship at the altar of Dolce Gabanna, an increasing number of people have turned to swelling church congregations around the country. Organised religion was essentially banned during the Soviet occupation and many priceless, centuries-old churches were converted to warehouses, gymnasiums and even planetariums. Today, they have been returned to their largely Lutheran, Catholic and Orthodox parishioners. The pagan religion of Latvia's ancestors has also been revived and demonstrations of folk life and religion play a large part in contemporary Latvian society.

Since 1991, Rigans have embraced the capitalist ideals of the Western world, and even though there have been some big winners and many more big losers, the citizens of Latvia's largest city are always willing to make a deal to ensure that their future is safe, free and prosperous. With the collapse of the so-called Evil Empire, their destiny is finally in their own hands.

● *Riga's citizens enjoy a beer on Dome Square*

Culture

Latvia has a rich and textured cultural life that includes music, theatre, festivals, films, museums and art galleries. The city is a true hub of culture in the Baltic area, and hardly a day passes without a renowned musician or performer making an appearance here. More importantly, since the end of the Soviet occupation in 1991, there has been a renaissance movement to restore Latvian culture.

Folk life, folk arts and folk music are an integral part of Latvian culture, and this is a country that doesn't simply celebrate its traditions, but elevates them to a pinnacle in every citizen's heart. The Latvian Song and Dance Festival draws thousands of performers, and even more spectators, every four years to a celebration of traditional music, art and costume (see page 8).

Opera is important to this city, and most of the soloists and performers of the Latvian National Opera were trained first at the Latvian Academy of Music and then continued their studies abroad before returning home. The Opera House has been restored to its former glory and its performances are praised by the international press for their originality and innovation.

Latvia, and Riga in particular, has been hailed as a bastion of ballet excellence. While in the domain of the Soviets, Riga was ranked third in importance as a ballet centre, after the Kirov and the Bolshoi. Over the years the Riga Ballet, officially known as the Ballet Company of the Latvian National Opera, has gained world renown through the performances of such stars as Mikhail Barishnikov, Aleksandr Godunov and Māris Liepa. The company performs both classical and modern works of choreography.

⦿ *Look upwards for striking art nouveau details on the city's buildings*

⬥ *Shostakovich's* The Bright Stream *is performed at the Latvian National Opera*

No less important are the theatre arts in Latvia. Theatre in Riga can trace its roots as far back as the 13th century. More recently, in the 1970s, the city was regarded as the hub of avant-garde productions, and the Riga New Theatre is the successor of that brave tradition.

Filmmaking has grown over the last few decades, mostly with documentary movies, many of which have won awards internationally. Latvians are devout film-goers and you'll find no shortage of newly-released films in the capital's cinemas.

And the museums. Ah, the museums. With more than 50 within the city of Riga, you'll never be short of things to see or do. History, the wars, maritime life, arts, decorative arts, medicine, writing, theatre, music, automobiles, telephones and railways all have their very own museum. Nothing you want on that list? There are also museums devoted to sport, photography, dolls, porcelain, architecture and even fire-fighting. It is within these museums, particularly the smaller and more specialised, that you will find Latvia through the eyes of the artists, inventors and citizens who have lived in this fascinating city.

⬥ *Despite wartime destruction, Riga remains an architectural delight*

MAKING THE MOST OF
Riga

Shopping

BEST BUYS

Let's cut to the chase. The first thing to buy is Laima chocolate, which can only be described as divinely decadent. Then try on some pieces of Baltic amber at any of the souvenir or antique shops in the Old Town. Chilly? Wrap yourself in a fashionable piece of Latvian linen, which is incredibly cheap compared to European prices. Then round off your shopping with a shot of the national drink, Riga Black Balsam, a liqueur made from herbs, flowers and medicinal roots. This is an acquired taste, but persevere; you can find it in most food and spirit shops. And there you have it, the complete Baltic food, drink and shopping experience.

WHERE TO SHOP

Shopping in Riga can be really expensive as consumer goods are inexplicably more highly priced than anywhere else in the Baltic, or Western Europe for that matter. However, if you must shop until you drop you'll find most of the best shops concentrated around the Old Town area and near the city centre. Modern shopping centres with dozens of shops, restaurants and supermarkets are also just a tram or trolleybus ride away.

However, you could try shopping at Origo, a shopping centre that straddles the renovated Central Station. Who would have imagined you could turn such a dull, but functional, space into a lively commercial arena? The world's your oyster here – get a computer part, drop off your dry cleaning, grab some flowers for your main squeeze and stop for a cocktail. There are hundreds of shops, cafés and services all within this one location.

Rigans buy special grasses and flowers to make wreaths for Midsummer's Eve

Near Central Station you'll find Central Market, housed in five enormous World War I-era zeppelin hangars; this is a bustling, noisy and aromatic place that you really should not miss. If they make it or grow it and it's legal you're sure to find someone selling it here. This is a perfect place to pick up the makings of an impromptu picnic. You can also find fake designer watches and Russian fur hats, but don't expect to find anything of real quality.

Can't live without a day spent crawling the mall? Each section of the city from the Old Town to the suburbs now has its own share of shopping centres. Galerija Centrs is now in the hands of a Norwegian firm that has successfully transformed the Soviet-style Universal department store into a Western mall with speciality shops, fast foods and a supermarket that now covers nearly an entire city block in Old Riga.

● Riga excels in handmade toys and gift items

Finland's most prestigious shopping centre, Stockmann (Ⓦ www.stockmann.lv), has also opened four floors of fashion and interior design accessories next to Riga train station. Best of all, it offers the finest supermarket in Latvia.

USEFUL SHOPPING PHRASES

What time do the shops open/close?
Cikos veikali tiek atvērti/slēgti?
Cik-os vake-ali tiek at-ver-ti/sleg-ti?

How much is this?
Cik tas maksā?
Tsik tas mak-saa?

Can I try this on?
Vai drīkstu šo pielaikot?
Vai dreek-stu sho peel-eye-kot?

Can you show me the one in the window/this one?
Vai variet man parādīt to, kas ir logā/šo?
Vai var-iet man pa-raa-deet toa, kas ir logaa/sho?

My size is...
Mans izmērs ir....
Mans iz-mers ir....

I'll take this one, thank you
Šo lūdzu, paldies
Sho loodz-u, paldies

Do you have anything cheaper/larger/smaller/ of better quality?
Vai jums ir kaut kas lētāks/lielāks/mazāks/kvalitatīvāks?
Vai yums ir kaut kas leht-aaks/leel-aaks/ maz-aaks/ kval-it-ta-teev-aaks?

Eating & drinking

Latvian cuisine is an adventure in cholesterol. Traditionally, Latvians are farmers who raise pigs, cows and other animals, so their diet is rich in meat and dairy products, with pork, cheese and sour cream involved in some manner with almost every dish. Bread holds a place of honour on the Latvian table, as it symbolises wealth.

Today in Riga, starters and snacks include: *rasols*, a salad of diced meat, herring, potatoes, peas, carrots and pickles, all glued together with sour cream and mayonnaise; *pīrāgi*, dough stuffed with cabbage and/or bacon bits; *pelmeņi*, a Russian version of ravioli; savoury pancakes filled with cheese or ham; potato pancakes; pork in aspic; smoked sausage; herring; smoked eel; and cabbage soup.

The local favourites to have with a round of beer are *pelēkie zirņi*, round, grey peas cooked with smoky bacon fat and onions, and *grauzdiņi*, black bread fried in garlic.

For the main course, the top of the local menu has specialities such as *karbonāde*, a chop or lightly breaded schnitzel, and *fileja*, a fillet of pork, beef or chicken. Cuts of pork and other meats traditionally come with a nice rind of fat around the edge, since serving lean meat is considered rude. Main dishes based on salmon and trout are also popular and main courses usually come with boiled potatoes or chips, coleslaw, and pickled vegetables. Garnishes include sour cream

PRICE CATEGORIES
Price ratings for restaurants in this book are based on the average cost of a main course for one person.
£ up to 5Ls **££** 5–10Ls **£££** over 10Ls

and mushroom sauce. Meals are normally served with white bread,
Latvian sourdough and dark rye bread.

USEFUL DINING PHRASES

I would like a table for ... people
Es vēlos galdu ... cilvēkiem
Es vehl-os gal-du ... cil-veh-kiem

Could I have it well-cooked/medium/rare please?
Man, lūdzu, labi izceptu/vidēji izceptu/asiņainu?
Man, loo-dzu, labi iz-tsep-tu/vid-eyi iz-tsep-tu/as-iny-eye-nu?

I am a vegetarian. Does this contain meat?
Es esmu veģetārietis. Vai tas ir ar gaļu?
Es esmu ved-yet-aar-eet-is. Vai tas ir ar gal-yu?

Where is the toilet (restroom) please?
Kur ir tualete?
Kur ir tu-al-ete?

I would like a beer/two beers, please
Man lūdzu vienu alu/divus alus, lūdzu
Man loo-dzu vie-nu alu/div-us alus, loo-dzu

Waiter! Waitress!	**May I have the bill please?**
Oficiant! Oficiante!	Rēķinu lūdzu!
Ofit-see-ant! Ofit-see-ante!	*Reht-yinu loo-dzu!*

A favourite Latvian dessert is *ķīselis*, an oat-porridge sweetened with seasonal fruit and berries. Other desserts include ice cream, tortes and cakes.

If the traditional Latvian food is too heavy for you, do not despair. In addition to dozens of smart restaurants and cafés offering international cuisine, Riga's dining scene is complimented by a wide variety of ethnic eateries that serve anything from sushi to tandoori.

On the liquid side, the Latvians prefer coffee during the day, and beer in the evening. Rigans frequent coffee shops in the daytime, and they normally take it black. If you want milk, ask for a *balta kafija* or a white coffee. Local chains such as Double Coffee have opened up dozens of coffee shops around town serving food, cocktails and excellent java and some are even open 24 hours. Beer normally comes as a regular lager, or as a dark porter, and the locals consume a lot of both. Although Aldaris and Cēsu are Latvia's largest breweries, Užavas, Tērvetes, Lāčplēsis and Bauskas are more traditional, unfiltered beers. The traditional Latvian spirit is the potent *Rīgas Melnais Balzams* or Riga Black Balsam, an acquired taste to say the least. Latvijas Balzams also produces nearly 50 different alcoholic beverages from brandies and whiskies to cream-based liqueurs which can be bought at its retail outlets. Thanks to the Russian influence, good, cheap vodka is also readily available.

Restorāns, meaning restaurant, indicates a more upmarket and expensive establishment, complete with starched white tablecloths and starched waiting staff. There are many of these in Riga, including in most major hotels. For something more informal, try a *krogs* or *krodziņš*, which is pub-like, often with rustic furnishings. At the bottom of the food chain are the *kafejnīcas*, which can range from greasy spoons to cafeterias and coffee houses. In the summer, Latvians prefer to have a drink at beer gardens or *alus dārzi*.

🔺 *Pick a trout or a sturgeon from the fishpond at Pie Kristapa Kunga (see page 99)*

Entertainment & nightlife

Riga is quickly gaining a reputation for having the liveliest nightlife in the Baltic region. The city is almost overflowing with discos, pubs and casinos. You'll have no difficulty finding something to suit your individual taste, from techno to house to jazz. And don't assume you have to be under 25 to enjoy Riga's night scene; you'll find plenty of hot spots for those with a bit of life left in the old zimmer.

If there's a national pastime in Latvia, it must be beer drinking. You can order a tasty brew nearly anywhere from cinemas to the gym and you can even drink a cold one in your car as long as you're not at the wheel. Although locals often prefer their own brands, many pubs also specialise in foreign beers, and some drinking establishments have more than 20 different beers on draught.

Filling out the beverage field of competitors is black balsam (see page 28), which can soothe the very hangovers it causes in the first place. If you make it out into the countryside, especially Latgale in eastern Latvia, be very wary of *kandža*, a traditional moonshine that is often inflicted on unsuspecting guests.

Nightlife in Riga is truly not so different from anywhere else. You can find large, noisy taverns filled with stag parties from the UK, or quiet, cosy cocktail bars. There are electric casinos and small blues clubs, as well as all sorts of other entertainment, from traditional live theatre to cutting-edge independent films at small art theatres.

Despite the influx of techno music and cheap drinking establishments, Riga remains a curiously formal place at night. If you are heading out to a club, eschew the sweat suits and trainers and at least make an attempt to be chic. If you're only interested in pubs and beer gardens then casual, comfortable clothes are fine.

● *Riga has plenty of trendy cocktail bars like Lounge 8 (see page 79)*

Sport & relaxation

Exercise, fitness and sports are big in Latvia, and its hockey, football, biathlon, marathon and even bobsleigh stars are held in the highest regard.

SPECTATOR SPORTS

Alongside winter sports, football generates a lot of passion in Latvia, with many players competing at local, national and international levels. The Latvian team surprised many when they qualified for the 2004 European Championships and even more when they held Germany to a 0-0 draw during the competition. Although local matches held in Riga at Skonto Stadium are still sparsely attended, international friendlies and qualifiers are often sold out. The stadium is about a 15-min walk from the Old Town, and tickets are available at the stadium on match days.

Skonto Stadium ⓐ Melngaila iela 1a, Riga ⓦ www.skontofc.lv

PARTICIPATION

Most major hotels offer exercise facilities and some even have swimming pools. The promenades along the Daugava, the green belts around the canal and city parks such as Mežaparks, are good for hiking and jogging. Riga has several clubs that offer aerobics, weight-lifting, yoga and other forms of fitness training. Facilities for basketball, billiards, cycling, horse riding, swimming, skating and tennis are also available.

At Sigulda, you can bungee jump over the Gauja river from a cable car. The height is about 45 m (148 ft). It operates during the summer months on Saturday and Sunday from 18.30 for 17–20Ls, but you should call and make an appointment before going.

LGK You can also take a run on the bobsleigh track at the weekend year round from 12.00–17.00 for about 5Ls per person. ☎ 26 44 06 60 Ⓦ www.lgk.lv.

EXERCISE & RELAXATION

If you absolutely, positively cannot go a day without working up a sweat with weights and cardio, don't despair. There are lots of health clubs, most offering aerobic classes, and a few of the larger chain hotels are equipped with swimming pools and exercise rooms. What else would you expect? Latvia may be a small country but it possesses hockey stars that play in the NHL and Jeļena Prokupčuka, who has won the New York marathon not once, but twice. And if aromatherapy, deep tissue massage and a pedicure are more of your idea of a workout, neither the city nor seashore locations will disappoint.

Yoga Centres

Daya Yoga Studio ⓐ Stabu iela 51/2 ☎ 67 27 61 04 Ⓦ www.joga.lv
Life Veda Institute Ayurvedic massage procedures from 9–30Ls.
ⓐ Barona iela 56 ☎ 67 29 89 51

Health Clubs

Atlantis Pool, sauna, hot tub, exercise and weight rooms.
ⓐ Lāčplēša iela 38 ☎ 67 28 08 70 Ⓦ www.atlantis.lv
City Fitness Pilates, ballet, spinning, rowing, weight room, sauna and massage. ⓐ Marijas iela 13 (Berga Bazārs)
☎ 67 28 85 85 Ⓦ www.cityfitness.lv
Joker Klubs ⓐ Katrīnas dambis 12 ☎ 67 09 98 00
Ⓦ www.jokerklubs.lv
Radisson Wellness Centre Pool, sauna, spa, hairdresser, exercise studio. ⓐ Radisson Hotel, Kuģu iela 24 ☎ 67 06 11 24

Accommodation

Riga has a wide range of hotels, bed and breakfasts, and loads of hostels, but many of these will take a significant chunk out of your budget. Latvia has not yet adopted the international 5-star standards so relying strictly on this as an indicator of the quality of the establishment may not be the best idea. Always be sure to ask what will be included with the room if items such as bathtubs or satellite TV service are a priority for your stay. Many low-budget hotels are former Soviet establishments and the furnishings and amenities usually haven't been updated for quite some time. Outside the city, guest houses or *viesu nami* are springing up like poppies after rain.

HOTELS

Hotel Enkurs ££ 'Hotel Anchor' is one of the few hotels in this ancient port city to sport a nautical theme. Although the life preservers and plastic crustaceans might not be to everyone's taste, the rooms are comfortable and offer satellite TV, mini-bar, phone, writing desk and private bathrooms. The suite also provides a sauna and a hot tub.
ⓐ Čaka iela 87 ❶ 67 84 63 40 ⓦ www.hotelenkurs.lv

Livonija ££ This small hotel located just beyond the Central Market is only a tram stop or two away from Old Riga. Although

PRICE CATEGORIES
The following price guides are based on the cost of a room for two people including breakfast, per night.
£ up to 20Ls   **££** 20–40Ls   **£££** 40–80Ls   **£££+** over 80Ls

the rooms aren't the biggest or most luxurious, people willing to forgo a mini-bar will appreciate the affordable prices.
🅐 Maskavas iela 32 📞 67 20 41 80 🅦 www.hotellivonija.lv
🅝 Tram: 7, 9 to Jēzusbaznīcas iela

Centra £££ Helpful, friendly staff, spacious rooms with minimalist décor and an enviable location on one of Old Riga's most popular streets make Centra a logical choice for people who enjoy style and comfort. Rooms on the upper floors also afford guests spectacular views of the Latvian capital's medieval heritage. 🅐 Audēju iela 1
📞 67 22 64 41 🅦 www.centra.lv

Europa City Hotel £££ The porthole windows and pronounced spacing of the floors of this hotel put one in mind of a ship. There is, however, no nautical theme, just tastefully decorated rooms with the usual amenities like cable TV and a top floor jazz and cocktail bar with an expansive summer terrace. 🅐 Brīvības iela 199c 📞 67 16 60 00
🅦 www.europacity.lv 🅝 Tram: 11 to VEF

Forums £££ Only a stone's throw from the bus station and Old Riga's best bars, Forums offers large rooms with satellite TV, writing desks and old-fashioned red and gold interiors. If you require a little more luxury, book the penthouse suite with its own sauna and private terrace. 🅐 Vaļņu iela 45 📞 67 81 46 80 🅦 www.hotelforums.lv

Hanza Hotel £££ Opened in 2007 in a renovated 19th-century building, Hanza Hotel is located on an historic square that has a unique octagonal church at its centre. All rooms are decorated in soothing earth tones and include the usual amenities, as well as heated tile floors in its bathrooms. A cellar pub and an upmarket

restaurant are also at your disposal. ⓐ Elijas iela 7 ⓣ 67 79 60 40
ⓦ www.hanzahotel.lv ⓝ Tram: 7, 9 to Jēzusbaznīcas

Kolonna Hotel Riga £££ Located on one of Old Riga's most picturesque
streets flanked by cafés and shops, this historic medieval building
now houses a surprisingly affordable hotel. Although each room
is slightly different, all provide cable TV, minimalist design and
en suite bathrooms. You can also reserve two-storey luxury suites.
ⓐ Tirgoņu iela 9 ⓣ 67 35 82 54 ⓦ www.hotelkolonna.lv

Konventa Sēta £££ The 'Convent Yard' consists of several medieval
buildings surrounding a central courtyard filled with good shopping
and eating and drinking opportunities. Although rooms vary in size
and décor, they all offer the standard amenities one would expect of
a good hotel. ⓐ Kalēju iela 9/11 ⓣ 67 08 75 01 ⓦ www.konventa.lv

Metropole £££ The oldest continuously-running hotel in Riga first
opened its doors in 1871. Although the smallish rooms reflect its
illustrious past, all include tasteful Scandinavian-style décor, satellite
TV, mini-bar, private bathrooms, wireless internet and trouser press.
Not surprisingly, its restaurant is one of the city's best. ⓐ Aspazijas
bulvāris 36/38 ⓣ 67 22 54 11 ⓦ www.metropole.lv

Reval Hotel Latvija £££ During the Soviet era all foreigners were
required to stay at this 27-storey skyscraper, where the rooms were
often bugged. Completely renovated, it's now a world-class hotel
and conference centre. Take advantage of the casino, its trendy
wine bar or the Skyline bar that offers the best views in the city.
ⓐ Elizabetes iela 55 ⓣ 67 77 22 22 ⓦ www.revalhotels.com

Albert Hotel £££+ A design hotel in its own right, this 11-storey skyscraper was created with the life and achievements of Albert Einstein in mind. Conference rooms are named 'Space' and 'Time'. 'Do not disturb' signs simply say 'I'm thinking' and the top-floor bar offers a summer terrace called Star Lounge. ⓐ Dzirnavu iela 33 ⓣ 67 33 17 17 ⓦ www.alberthotel.lv

Avalon Hotel £££+ What appears to be a big glass box on the edge of Old Riga is actually an excellent hotel with a bright courtyard atrium

▶ *Boutique hotels have replaced aging Soviet edifices*

and over 100 stylishly-decorated rooms with flat screen cable TVs, mini-bar, wireless internet, safe, en suite bathrooms and even ironing boards. A sixth-floor smoking terrace is also available as well as an upmarket restaurant. ⓐ Kalēju iela 70/72 ⓣ 67 16 99 99 ⓦ www.hotelavalon.eu

Europa Royale Riga £££+ Once a mansion owned by a 19th-century publishing magnate, this elegant building has been transformed into an upmarket hotel. Nearly all of its old world charm has been preserved from the intricate parquet floors and stained glass windows to the original tile fireplaces and crystal chandeliers. All rooms are a mix of antique opulence and modern conveniences. ⓐ Barona iela 12 ⓣ 67 07 94 44 ⓦ www.europaroyale.com

Hotel Bergs £££+ Recently named by Conde Naste Traveler as one of the world's top 100 design hotels, Bergs offers 38 spacious suites decorated in a minimalist style using natural, local materials. Its restaurant is also one of the best Riga has to offer. ⓐ Elizabetes iela 83/85 ⓣ 67 77 09 00 ⓦ www.hotelbergs.lv

Reval Hotel Rīdzene £££+ Originally built as a luxurious hotel for visiting Communist Party elites, it's now a luxurious hotel for anyone who can afford to stay here. Spacious, tastefully decorated rooms surround a capacious atrium and the prominent security detail at the US Embassy next door should guarantee a safe stay. ⓐ Reimersa iela 1 ⓣ 67 32 44 22 ⓦ www.revalhotels.com

BED & BREAKFAST
Homestay £–££ This bright and inviting home in the Mežaparks district, run by a Latvian-New Zealand couple, is both comfy and

hospitable. Guests have access to the kitchen, the living room with its multi-channel television, English books in every room, and a shower with skylights. ⓐ Stokholmas iela 1 ⓣ 67 55 30 16 ⓦ www.homestay.lv ⓝ Tram: 11, or call to arrange transport

KB £–££ Run by a relative of Krišjānis Barons, the revered folk song collector after whom the street and the B&B are named, KB provides bright, affordable rooms with cable TV and en suite bathrooms as well as a communal kitchen and free internet access. The top-floor apartment can accommodate several people and has a fantastic private terrace. ⓐ Barona iela 37 ⓣ 67 31 23 23 ⓦ www.kbhotel.lv

Multilux ££ One of Riga's first proper B&Bs, Multilux offers renovated rooms with standard amenities such as cable TV and private bathrooms as well as a laundry service and airport transfer. It also boasts a central location, roughly a 15-minute walk from Old Riga. ⓐ Barona iela 37 (entrance from Ģertrūdes) ⓣ 67 31 16 02 ⓦ www.multilux.lv

HOSTELS
Profitcamp £ The dorm beds are clean and cheap, and there's a communal kitchen, laundry machines and internet. This is basic done brilliantly. ⓐ Teātra iela 12 ⓣ 67 21 63 61 ⓦ www.profitcamp.lv.

Riga Old Town Hostel £ This cosy hostel located in Old Riga, not far from the bus and train stations, was the first of its genre to open in the Latvian capital. Beds in any of its dorms are clean and comfortable and perks include in-room safes, wireless internet access, The Backpackers Bar and no curfew. ⓐ Vaļņu iela 43 ⓣ 67 22 34 06 ⓦ www.rigaoldtownhostel.lv

THE BEST OF RIGA

TOP 10 ATTRACTIONS

These are sights you should try not to miss on any trip to Riga.

- **Art nouveau architecture** Can't get enough of caryatids and nymphs adorning the architecture? You'll revel in the well-preserved buildings of Riga's art nouveau district, one of the biggest collections in Europe (see pages 86–90)

- **Central Market** On its completion in 1930, Riga's Central Market was the largest and most modern in Europe. Visit it to sample an authentic slice of Latvian life (see page 90)

- **Dome Cathedral** The largest place of worship in the Baltics and housing one of the biggest pipe organs in Europe (see page 66)

- **Gauja National Park** A spectacularly beautiful national park only an hour's drive or train trip from Riga. Bungee jump, hit the bobsleigh track or drift down the River Gauja in a canoe (see pages 117–19)

- **House of the Blackheads** Weird name, but this reconstructed medieval edifice is the showpiece of the Old Town (see pages 69–70)

- **Jūrmala** This stretch of seashore, only a short distance from Riga, is the bucket-and-spade paradise of Latvia (see pages 120–29)

- **Old Town** Eight centuries of history crammed into a charming chaos of narrow streets adorned with outdoor cafés, intriguing architecture and ultra-hip nightlife (see pages 60–81)

- **Open-air Ethnographic Museum** Spend a while in an atmosphere of days gone by in this vast ensemble of timber-built farmhouses garnered from all regions of the country (see page 93)

- **Rundāle Palace** This sumptuous palace, stuffed with restored 18th-century furnishings, was designed by Rastrelli, renowned architect of the Winter Palace in St. Petersburg (see page 133)

- **St Peter's Church** A graceful three-tiered spire adorns this red-brick church. Take the lift to the top for a jaw-dropping view of the Old Town and environs (see page 73)

◐ *Old Riga's famous red roofs from above*

Suggested Itineraries

Here's a quick guide to seeing the best of Riga, depending on the time available.

HALF-DAY: RIGA IN A HURRY

If your time for sightseeing is limited to only a few hours, you are in luck. Riga, especially the historic Old Town, is quite compact, with many of the city's top attractions bunched quite close together. Start at Rātslaukums (Town Hall Square) and visit the Blackheads House and the Occupation Museum. Go across the square and take the lift up to the top of St Peter's, ending your tour at the cathedral on Doma laukums.

1 DAY: TIME TO SEE A LITTLE MORE

With a whole day to spare, you can widen your horizons after the whistle-stop tour suggested above, and explore more of Riga's historic centre. Don't miss picturesque Skārņu iela and St John's Church, the guildhalls on Līvu laukums, the Powder Tower, the Swedish Gate and, finally, Riga Castle.

2–3 DAYS: TIME TO SEE MUCH MORE

If you have more than one day, and have been concentrating on the Old Town, you should take a look at some of the other things Riga has to offer. If you want to slow down the pace, try exploring the city's parks, beyond Brīvības bulvāris and the Freedom Monument. If you haven't already investigated the city's art nouveau architecture, follow our itinerary on pages 88–90 around the small area near Elizabetes iela that has the greatest concentration of art nouveau buildings in the city, if not the world. If you enjoy things mechanical, try the Latvian Railway Museum (about 1 km across the Akmens bridge on the opposite side of the river) or the Motor Museum (see page 93), also a little way out of town. For those with green fingers, Riga has the Botanical Gardens in Pārdaugava and Salaspils, the site of the Latvian National Botanical Gardens.

LONGER: ENJOYING RIGA TO THE FULL

If you find yourself with at least a week in Riga, you should consider travelling out to see more of Latvia on one or two of our suggested Out of Town trips. Just west of Riga is Jūrmala (Seashore), a collection of small beach resorts scattered along about 20 km (12 miles) of the Baltic coastline. This is a good half-day excursion, or you can arrange a hotel room and spend a whole day at the beach.

Bauska is about 75 km (46 miles) south of Riga. The ruins of Bauska Castle, currently undergoing reconstruction, are worth a visit, while 13 km (8 miles) west is Rundāle Palace, a magnificent baroque structure filled with antique furnishings; 10 km (6 miles) northwest is Mežotne Palace, a neo-classical building that is now a hotel. You should plan on a full day to see all three sites.

In the east of Latvia are the Gauja Valley, with the Gauja National Park, and the towns of Sigulda, Cēsis and Valmiera. The area is also laced with the remains of old Livonian castles, churches and museums. It would easily take two or three days to explore it and its natural beauty completely.

To the west are the Baltic Coast, and the towns of Kuldīga (the prettiest of the provincial towns in Latvia) and seaside Ventspils and Liepāja. If there has been a recent storm, look for amber washed up on the seashore. This is at least a two-day trip, but you may want to take longer.

Something for nothing

You don't have to spend a fortune to enjoy much of what Riga has to offer. Here are just a few ideas for getting the most out of a visit without denting your wallet.

Brāļu kapi (Brethren Cemetery)
The brainchild of Latvian sculptor Kārlis Zāle, who also designed the Freedom Monument, this is truly one of the most striking memorials in Latvia. It was built as a tribute to the nation's soldiers who perished in World War I. ⓐ Bērzu aleja ⓝ Tram: 11 to Brāļu kapi

Central Market
Each of its five zeppelin hangars specialises in either meat, fish, dairy products, fruit and vegetables or cereals. You can walk around for hours watching burly men with cleavers or just sample what the stocky women in aprons have to offer. You can usually get free samples of cheese and even fruit if the hawkers think you might actually buy something. Look out for a local delicacy called *kaņepu sviests* or simply hemp butter ⓦ www.centraltirgus.lv

🔺 Livs' Square is always a good place to take a well-deserved beer break

Kara muzejs (War Museum)
Since the late 12th century, the land that is now Latvia has been attacked by Teutonic crusaders, Polish and Swedish kings, Russian tsars, Soviet troops and the Nazis, to name just a few. This museum attached to the historic Powder Tower focuses on the wars fought on Latvian soil during the 20th century, and chronicles the birth and development of the Latvian armed forces. ⓐ Smilšu iela 20 ⓣ 67 22 81 47 ⓦ www.karamuzejs.lv

Ķemeri National Park
Although it will cost you a couple of Lats to take the train to the far end of Jūrmala, the dozens of sign-posted nature trails throughout this protected ecosystem are free. Stroll along boardwalks above the incredible swamps, lakes and raised bogs of Ķemeri that provide shelter for hundreds of unique species of wildlife including rare black storks, wild cattle, elk, moose, foxes and even wolves ⓦ www.kemeri.gov.lv

Latvijas okupācijas muzejs (Museum of Latvia's Occupation)
This museum is worthy of an admission price any day, so take advantage of this freebie. The various exhibits display the atrocities committed against the Latvian people. You can even walk into a reconstruction of a gulag barracks and get a sense of the intolerable living conditions of a Siberian labour camp (see pages 62 & 67).

Latvijas vēstures muzejs (Latvian History Museum)
On Wednesdays wander through halls of history here – it's free! And you'll learn a little bit about Latvian history to boot (see page 67).

Vecrīga (Old Riga)
There is no charge for the history that you cannot help but absorb as you wander the chaotic mass of streets and statuary (see pages 60–81).

When it rains

Riga may be one of the best cities in which to spend a drizzly day, which is a very good thing because it certainly does drizzle a lot here in the spring and autumn. Fortunately, there are enough museums and cinemas to satisfy cravings for an historic or contemporary culture fix. The smaller museums reveal a close-up look at the Latvian personality and the need to document, it would seem, everything. Here are some of the most eclectic.

Mentzendorff House (see page 70) offers an idea of how wealthy Rigans lived in the 17th and 18th centuries. Once owned by a rich merchant, this museum provides a glimpse of the day-to-day life of that era, including period furniture and original wall frescoes.

The creepy-crawlies at the **Museum of Nature** (see page 91) include everything from specimens from the Cretaceous era to pickled body parts and stuffed animals. It also has the best collection of fossilised fish in the former USSR.

The impressive exterior of **House of the Blackheads** is matched by the opulent rooms inside (see page 69).

Rīgas vēstures un kuģniecības muzejs (Riga's History and Navigation Museum) offers trinkets, memorabilia and fine art from the Bronze Age to the 20th century. It also provides great views of the Dome Cloister in the courtyard (see page 71).

Rīgas Motormuzejs (Riga Motor Museum) Can't get enough of chrome and running boards? Spend an afternoon away from the city centre in this exhibition of classic cars. Lincolns, Mercedes and BMWs as well as vehicles owned by Stalin and Brezhnev are all garaged together along with some motorcycles (some with sidecars) from days gone by (see page 93).

🔺 *The interior of the House of Blackheads is nearly as impressive as its façade*

On arrival

TIME DIFFERENCE

Latvia is 2 hours ahead of Greenwich Mean Time (GMT) and 3 hours ahead during daylight saving.

ARRIVING

By air

Riga International Airport is located 10km (6 miles) southwest of Riga centre. The airport was given an award for being the best airport of its size in the EU and was recently expanded. It has a full range of services from money exchange, tourist information, banks, internet services, post office, rental car services, shops and restaurants.

Bus no. 22 goes to the city centre (Strēlnieku laukums and the train station) and leaves every 20–30 minutes. The cost is 0.30Ls.

You can order a taxi from a desk in the arrivals hall, or you can simply go outside and hail one from a queue outside the arrivals hall. A typical ride to Old Riga or the city centre should cost no more than 10Ls. All of the red mini-van taxis at the airport are reputable and reliable, but you should always order a taxi by phone once in Riga. Some hotels provide a free shuttle service from the airport.

Riga International Airport Ⓦ www.riga-airport.com

By rail

The main railway station is located adjacent to the south end of the Old Town, in the city centre. There are separate arrival and departure lounges for domestic and international services. The station has essentially been transformed into a shopping centre with ATMs, banks, currency exchanges, information offices, ticket booths, shops and restaurants. Avoid the dodgy taxis outside the station.

Central Railway Station (Centrālā stacija) ⓐ Stacijas laukums
ⓣ 1181, 67 23 11 81 ⓦ www.ldz.lv

By road

Riga is served by highways to the north, east and south. Highway E67 goes north to Estonia, and south to Lithuania; Highway E77 and Highway E22 both go east to Russia; and Highway A6 goes southeast to Belarus. Although the highways have improved since EU membership and the public works bonanza that followed, a highway is rarely better than a narrow, potholed, two-laned road stretching in either direction.

Speed limits are 50 kmh (32 mph) in towns, 70 kmh (44 mph) in suburbs, 90 kmh (56 mph) on open roads, and 100 kmh (62 mph) on highways. As in the rest of continental Europe, driving is on the right-hand side. Seat-belt use is mandatory. There is zero tolerance for the use of alcohol while driving, and use of mobile phones while driving is also forbidden. Drunk drivers face a mandatory ten-day jail sentence. It is also compulsory to drive with headlights on. Foreign drivers are required to have a national licence, an International Driving Permit, registration documents, and proof of insurance.

Riga is connected by bus lines to most major cities in Europe. The bus station is located on the Riga Canal at the south end of the Old Town. It has ticket booths, currency exchanges, ATMs, a pharmacy, several kiosks and news-stands, a cafeteria and bar on the top floor and even a small hotel often used by bus drivers. The railway station is only a five-minute walk to the northeast. Trams 7 and 9 stop in front of the bus station, and will take you into the centre of town for 0.30Ls. Taxis are also available outside, but they're not recommended.

Riga International Bus Station (Autoosta) ⓐ Prāgas iela 1 ⓣ 900 00 09
ⓦ www.autoosta.lv

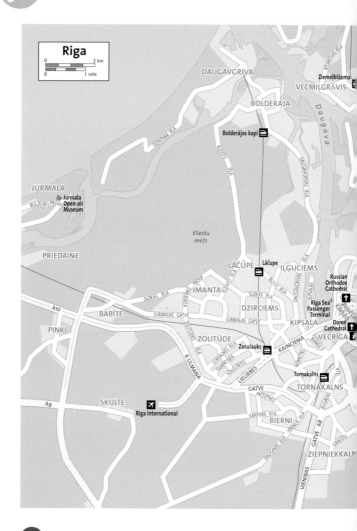

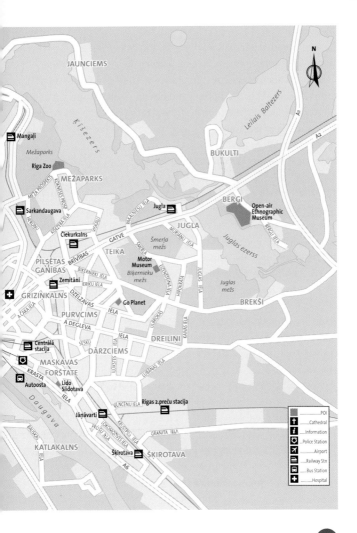

By water

There are limited international ferry services from Lübeck in Germany, and daily services from Stockholm, Sweden. Riga's Sea Passenger Terminal is about 1 km from the Old Town. The terminal has an ATM, currency exchange, a restaurant and not much else. Trams 5, 7 or 9 all stop in front of the terminal, and will take you to the city centre for 0.30Ls. Taxis are available outside the terminal, but insist on an agreed fare before leaving.

Riga Sea Passenger Terminal ⓐ Eksporta iela 3a ① 67 32 62 00.

FINDING YOUR FEET

If you are going to be in Riga for one to three days, and plan to see as many sights as possible, buy a **Riga Card**. A sightseeing tour, entrance to most cultural and tourist attractions, and entry or at least discounts to most museums are included in the price of the card. You can also use it as a transport ticket on trams, buses and trolleybuses. Some merchants also offer discounts on goods and services to holders of valid Riga Cards. The cost of the card is 8Ls for 24 hours, 12Ls for 48 hours, and 16Ls for 72 hours. Children under the age of 16 are half-price. If, however, you're not interested in the free bus tour included in the price and don't mind buying individual tickets for transport and museums, then it's not an absolute necessity.

You can buy the Riga Card at the **Riga Tourist Information Centre** ⓐ Rātslaukums 6, or online at ⓦ www.inyourpocket.com. Information is available at ⓦ www.rigacard.lv.

Make your first stop the tourist information centre in the Old Town. It offers a wide range of information in a variety of languages and can assist with hotel bookings and other useful services.

City of Riga Information Centre ⓐ Rātslaukums 6 ① 67 03 79 00
① 67 03 79 10 ⓦ www.rigatourism.com

The Latvian economy is booming and Riga is at its epicentre. Despite this, wealth is still concentrated among the few, with many residents struggling to make ends meet: petty theft can be a problem. Sneak thieves and pickpockets are also common, especially in areas frequented by tourists, so be careful. Visitors are advised not to carry large sums of cash, and not to flaunt expensive jewellery, cameras or electronic equipment.

Traffic in Riga is bad, and the driving tends to be aggressive and definitely not pedestrian-friendly. You need to be careful when crossing streets. Drunken driving is also common.

The pace of life is quite hectic, especially in the Old Town. Here, the narrow winding streets, although not conducive to cars, are open to anyone who has a permit or who has paid the steep fee to enter Old Riga. Pedestrians may officially have the right of way and many a group of retired tourists has brought traffic to a standstill, but Latvia's aggressive drivers often think the opposite is true so beware of BMWs with tinted windows.

English is widely spoken in Latvia by most people under the age of 40. There is one English-language newspaper in Latvia; *The Baltic Times* is published weekly, and is available at most hotels, some restaurants, and many news-stands. Other English-language publications are shipped into Riga, and, again, are available at most major hotels, and at many news-stands. For local events and other useful information in English pick up a copy of *Riga In Your Pocket*, the city's best local guide.

ORIENTATION

Riga sits on the Daugava River. The eastern, or right bank, holds most of the city's interesting areas. The historic heart of the city, the Old Town (Old Riga or Vecrīga), is about 1.5 km (1 mile) long by about 1 km (0.6 miles) wide, and is surrounded by the Daugava River to the southwest, and by the Pilsētas kanāls (City Canal) to the northwest.

11 Novembra krastmala is a wide street that separates the Old Town from the river. Its charming pedestrian walkway is a departure point for riverboats in the summer. The skyline of the Old Town is dominated by several spires: St Jacob's Church, the Dome Cathedral, the clock tower of the Town Hall, St Peter's Church and St. Saviour's to name just a few.

The Old Town is bisected by Kaļķu iela. About a block from the river on Kaļķu iela is Rātslaukums, or Town Hall Square. The Rātsnams (Town Hall), the Blackheads House, the Museum of Latvia's Occupation, and a very good tourist information office are all located at here. The main railway station and the main international bus terminal are on the southeast edge of the Old Town.

The rest of the 'new' city radiates outwards from the Old Town. At the Canal, Kaļķu becomes Brīvības bulvāris. Nearly one third of all buildings in this area are art nouveau in style. The western, or left, bank of the Daugava River offers noteworthy sights such as the massive Soviet Victory Monument, some impressive churches and the Latvian Railway Museum.

An outstanding place to get a sense of Riga is from atop the sky-scraping Reval Hotel Latvija at Elizabetes iela 55; by looking out of the tall windows on both sides of the eagle's nest Skyline Bar, you can see the whole of the city.

GETTING AROUND

On foot, Riga is quite compact, with most major attractions within 1 km (0.6 miles) of the City Centre and Old Town, so walking is

IF YOU GET LOST, TRY ...

Excuse me, do you speak English?
Atvainojiet, vai jūs runājiet angliski?
At-vine-oi-iet, vai yoos ru-naa-yiet an-gli-ski?

Excuse me, is this the right way to the cathedral/the tourist information office/the castle/the old town?
Atvainojiet, vai šis ir pareizais ceļš uz katedrāli/tūristu informācijas biroju/pili/vecpilsētu?
At-vine-oi-yiet, vai shis ir pa-rays-ice celysh uz ka-te-draali/tooristu infor-maat-see-yas bi-roy-u/pi-li/vets-pil-sad-u?

Can you point to it on my map?
Vai jūs varat to parādīt kartē?
Vai yoos var-at to pa-rod-eet kar-te?

a practical and viable option, and generally more fun than using public transport. The maps in this book are up to date and will help you navigate the main streets, but Riga's street system is complex and a detailed map obtained locally will be invaluable.

Public transport
Riga has an extensive network of trams, buses, trolleys and local trains. The cost is only 0.30Ls for any one trip, but there are no transfers. Tickets may be purchased from the driver or conductor or, for trams, at most kiosks.

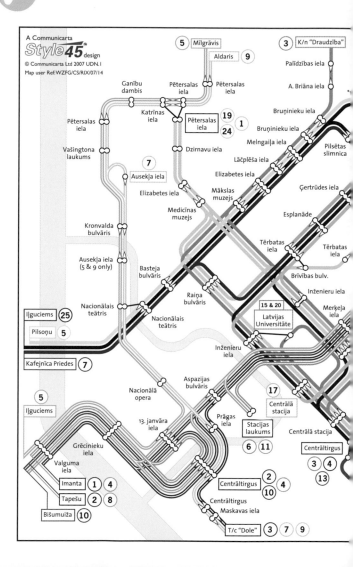

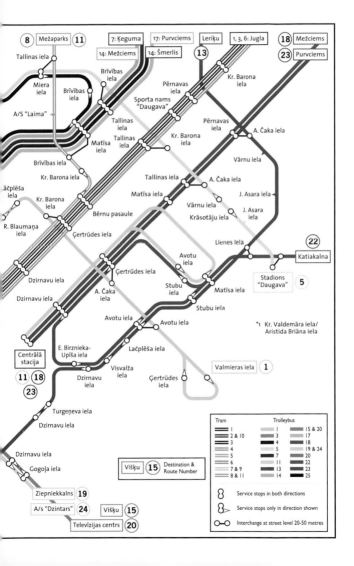

Taxis

There are several taxi companies in Riga, and although it is easy to flag down a taxi, it's not recommended. Dodgy cabs are common so order a taxi by phone to avoid being ripped off. Reputable taxis are **Rigas Taksometru Parks** (☎ 800 1313), which are also available at the airport and Reval Hotel Latvija; **Lady Taxi** (☎ 27 80 90 00), which only employs female drivers; and **Smile Taxi** (☎ 67 26 25 25). A taxi ride to and from any point inside the city centre/Old Town area should cost about 3L to 5L. Rates are slightly higher at night. Many taxis now accept most major credit cards, so look for your card's sticker in the window. Bear in mind that taxis must also pay to enter Old Riga, so you might want to ask them to drop you off somewhere just outside.

Car hire

Unless you are planning on visiting locations well outside Riga, renting a car is not recommended. The city is so compact, with most of the attractions close enough, that walking, using public transport, or even hiring taxis, is much more economical and practical. However most of the major car rental agencies are represented in Riga, both at the airport, and in the city centre. You can expect to pay the same prices as in Western Europe. There are some local car rental companies that can be cheaper than the major renters and well worth a try. Here then is a list of both big and small companies:

Auto Offers new cars and even driver services ☎ 29 58 04 48
🌐 www.carsrent.lv

Europcar ☎ 67 22 26 37 🌐 www.europcar.lv

Hertz ☎ 67 22 42 23 🌐 www.hertz.lv

Sixt – Baltic Car Lease ☎ 67 20 71 21 🌐 www.sixt.lv

▶ *The sprawling Central Market lies just beyond the Old Town*

THE CITY OF
Riga

Old Town

The Old Town or Vecrīga, the historic and geographic centre of the city, is located on the right bank of the Daugava River. Over 800 years old, it contains a unique collection of architectural monuments and buildings. A walk through its cobble-stoned streets will allow you see 19th-century art nouveau masterpieces as well as medieval churches and squares.

Start at Rātslaukums (Town Hall Square), where you get to see four sights in one. First is the House of the Blackheads. This building is a reconstruction of the original structure, which was completely destroyed in World War II. Riga's main tourist office is located here and can give you maps and other information to make the rest of your sightseeing easier. You can also buy your Riga Card here.

The House of the Blackheads was started in the 14th century as a guild for unmarried merchants and quickly evolved into a powerful political entity that was known throughout the Baltic for its bacchanalian debauchery. Today, chamber concerts are held in the main hall. Call that progress?

Across the street is Rātsnams (Town Hall). Rebuilt by the Russians after World War II as a Soviet-style block, its reconstruction was based on its original 18th-century design, with a few extras such as a glass roof and subterranean atrium. Its façade and clock tower still look like the genuine article.

On the square between Rātsnams and the House of the Blackheads is a statue of Roland, the legendary 8th-century knight who was killed fighting the Moors in a battle for control of a Pyrenean mountain pass. The first statue was erected in the 19th century on this same spot, but was removed after it was damaged during World War II. The current version is a replica.

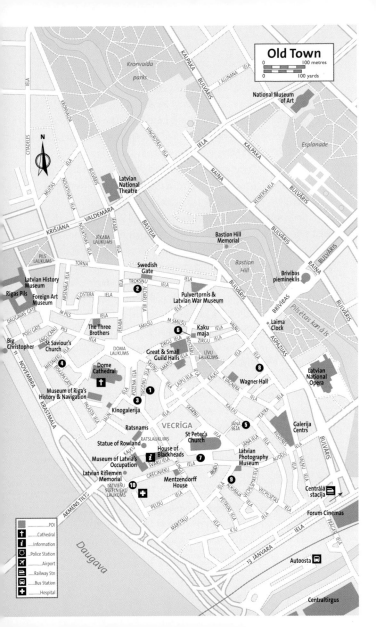

On the west side of Rātslaukums is the rear of the Museum of Latvia's Occupation. It is a forbidding Soviet structure, which contrasts sharply with the colourful buildings around it. The museum was built by the Soviets to honour the Red Riflemen, a group of Latvian soldiers who fought bravely for the Bolsheviks during the Russian Civil War, some of whom became Lenin's personal guard. Since the regaining of independence, the museum has been converted to show the horrors endured by the Latvians at the hands of both the Nazis and Soviets since the beginning of World War II. Entry is on the west side of the building off Strēlnieku laukums (Riflemen's Square). The square also has an impressive red granite monument dedicated to all Latvian riflemen – both communist and nationalist forces.

From Rātslaukums, walk east in front of the House of the Blackheads, cross Kungu iela, and you will be at St Peter's Church. This large red brick church has a graceful three-tiered spire, which is the city's trademark symbol. The original spire was built in 1491, but collapsed 200 years later and has been rebuilt and destroyed several times, most recently by a stray artillery shell in 1941. The current spire is 123 m (403 ft) high and has an internal lift, which will take you to an observation tower for an impressive view of the entire city.

Due east of St Peter's Church, on Skārņu iela, is St John's Church. Built in the 13th century, the red brick gable looks best in the afternoon sun. The Gothic interior has recently been painted in bright primary colours. Two chilling masks can be seen on the façade; they represent two monks who were voluntarily walled up inside the church, supposedly as an act of penance.

Moving northwest on Skārnu iela, you come to the 13th-century chapel of St George, which now houses the Museum of Decorative Art and Design, which displays such things as weaving, glassware, pottery and tableware.

⬤ *The best way to see Old Riga's towering spires is from a riverboat*

Continue on Skārnu iela, turn right on Kaļķu iela and left one block later onto Meistaru iela. This brings you to Līvu laukums, where you will find clustered together two buildings known as the Great Guild and Small Guild. The neo-Gothic Great Guild was given its current appearance in the 19th century, and now serves as a venue for performances of the Latvian National Symphony Orchestra. The Small Guild is more interesting, being asymmetrical with a turret on one side and a spire on the other. Facing the guilds is a yellow building in art nouveau style, with cats decorating its two turrets, and hence called the Cat House.

Continuing north on Meistaru, you will come to the Pulvertornis, or Powder Tower. This red-brick bastion was built in the 14th century. Its walls are embedded with cannonballs from various sieges and it is now part of the Latvian War Museum.

From the north side of the Powder Tower, go west on Torņa iela. The long building on the north side of the street is Jacobs's Barracks. Originally built by the Swedes in the 17th century, it now contains offices and upmarket shops. At Aldaru iela you will see the Swedish

---

PILSĒTAS KANĀLS

The Old Town was a fortified city for many years, with a moat around it. In the middle of the 19th century, it was decided it was no longer necessary to fortify the city, and many buildings and ramparts were dismantled. With so much open area, green spaces, and parks 300 m (984 ft) wide or more, were created on both sides of the canal. Public buildings were also added to the area. Today this space provides an oasis in the middle of this modern and growing city.

Gate. It is a simple archway beneath a large house, and is the only surviving city gate. It no longer goes anywhere in particular, but the alleys on the other side make an interesting side trip.

Continuing along Torņa iela, you will come to Jēkaba laukums. Across from the square is the Arsenal Gallery, which features high-profile contemporary art shows. Torņa iela ends at Pils laukums, the site of Rīgas Pils (Riga Castle). Originally built in the 14th century as headquarters for the Livonian Order, the castle has been through several alterations. Today it is the office of the Latvian president, as well as the home of two museums, the Foreign Art Museum and the Latvian History Museum. From the south end of Pils laukums, go east on Mazā Pils iela. Here you will find three interesting buildings known as the Three Brothers. The oldest on the right dates back to the 15th century and appears to be falling over. The second brother, from the 16th century, in the middle, is painted yellow, and has an interesting portal. It houses the Latvian Architecture Museum. The third brother on the left is rather unassuming, and painted green. At the end of Mazā Pils iela, turn right on Jēkaba iela, and you will come to Doma laukums (Dome Square).

Doma laukums is the core of the Old Town, and a good place to end a half-day tour. The square is dominated by Riga's Romanesque cathedral; begun in 1211, it is the biggest cathedral in the Baltics. It is magnificent both inside and out. The cathedral features a huge organ (within 6768 pipes) constructed in the 19th century. The largest in the world when built, it is now ranked fourth-largest.

SIGHTS & ATTRACTIONS

Anglikāņu baznīca (St Saviour's Church)

A little piece of Britain in Riga's old town. This Gothic-style church was built in 1857 on 10 m of gravel brought from Britain by a group of English merchants. Services are still conducted in English every Sunday at 11.00. ❸ Anglikāņu 2a

Ārzemju mākslas muzejs (Foreign Art Museum)

This museum houses the largest collection of foreign art in Latvia, with works dating back to the 15th century. Highlights include works of German and Dutch masters from the 17th to 19th centuries. ❸ Pils laukums 3❶ 67 22 64 67 ❺ 11.00–17.00, closed Mon. Admission charge

Doma baznīca (Dome Cathedral)

The largest church in Latvia was constructed over several centuries, beginning in 1211, and its architecture reflects a varied mix of early Gothic, baroque and Romanesque styles, among others. Despite the many influences, the structure has an eclectic flair that enchants the eye. The inside of the Cathedral is chock-a-block with plaques commemorating Latvia's medieval rulers. The huge church organ was installed in 1884. It was such a momentous occasion that Franz Lizst was commissioned to write a piece of music in its honour. Grab a schedule at the entrance or tourist office and make a point of hearing a concert. ❸ Doma laukums 1 ❶ 67 21 32 13 ❿ www.doms.lv ❺ 10.00–18.00. Admission charge

Kaķu māja (Cat House)

Rejected from a guild? Want to get even? Commission a pair of statuary cats to perch atop your roof with their backsides positioned in the direction of those who rejected you. That's the course the owner of this house took to show his displeasure at being turned down for guild membership. The guild viewed this action as the insult it was meant to be and sued in court to have the animals shifted to a less offensive position. They finally settled. ➌ Meistaru iela 19

Latviešu strēlnieku piemineklis (Latvian Riflemen Memorial)

In the heart of the Old Town stands a somewhat controversial statue honouring the Latvian Red Riflemen, some of who became the personal guards of Lenin. Some residents of the city see this monument as a symbol of the Soviet occupation and yearn to tear it down. Others see it as a tribute to the Latvians who fought in the early years of World War I. Regardless of which side you take, it is an impressive statue. ➌ Strēlnieku laukums

Latvijas okupācijas muzejs (Museum of Latvia's Occupation)

Once solely devoted to honouring the Latvian Red Riflemen, the building now houses a museum dedicated to the Nazi and Soviet occupations of Latvia. Various exhibits display the atrocities committed against the people of Latvia and the attempted systematic destruction of the nation's sovereignty. Visitors can walk into a reconstruction of a gulag barrack and glimpse the intolerable living conditions of those cruelly sentenced to one of these labour camps. ➌ Strēlnieku laukums 1 ➋ 67 21 27 15 ➌ 11.00–17.00, closed Mon. Free admission

Latvijas vēstures muzejs (Latvian History Museum)

View the evolution of Latvia and its people from the Stone Age to the present. Themed exhibits include ancient times, medieval Riga, the lifestyle of the peasants and upper classes in the 18th and 19th centuries, the foundation of the Latvian Republic and the occupation by the Soviets. Tours are available in English but must be booked in advance. ➋ 67 22 13 57 ➌ 11.00–17.0, closed Mon & Tues. Admission charge (free on Wed)

Lielā un Mazā ģilde (Great & Small Guild Halls)

The Great Guild Hall was once home to Riga's power brokers, the merchants, while the Small Guild was for the city's artisans. Today these two 14th-century buildings are venues for musical performances. The Great Guild is home to the Latvian Symphony Orchestra and the smaller cousin hosts contemporary performances and conferences.
ⓐ Amatu iela 6 & 5

Latvian Symphony Orchestra ☎ 67 21 36 43

Lielais Kristaps (Big Christopher)

Legend has it that Big Christopher, the protector of the city from floods and other natural disasters, first appeared in the 16th century in a small cave in a bank of the Daugava River. For centuries Latvians have paid tribute to this gentle giant with flowers and lit candles, asking for his blessing before departing on a long journey. In modern times his statue was moved to the safety of the Museum of Riga's History and Navigation. Today, a full-sized replica encased in glass stands guard over the river. ⓔ Poļu Gāte and 11 Novembra krastmala

Melngalvju nams (House of the Blackheads)

This is one of the best-known architectural treasures of Riga. Original construction began in the 14th century on the two buildings that comprise an asymmetrical and somewhat incongruous structure. The building boasts enormous stepped gables, ornately framed windows and niches filled with statuary. Initially it was used as a meeting place for many of Riga's guilds. Eventually it became associated with just one group – the unmarried merchants who took the name Blackheads in honour of their patron St Maurice, a Roman warrior of North African

◖ *St Maurice guards one side of the entrance to the House of the Blackheads*

origin. Over the centuries the building was the scene of rowdy, grandiose feasts such as Fasnachtsdrunken (Carnival Drinking Bout), Shrovetide celebrations, debuts of musical works and theatrical events. Very nearly bombed into extinction during World War II, the buildings have been meticulously restored to their former glory.

The Blackheads survived as an organisation until 1940, when the last of its members moved to Germany as part of Hitler's repatriation programme. Today the House fulfils a social role in the city, serving as a venue for chamber music concerts, and sharing ground-level space with the Riga tourist office and a café styled in the opulence of the 19th century. ⓐ Rātslaukums 7 ⓣ 67 04 43 00 ⓛ 10.00–17.00, closed Mon. Admission charge

Mencendorfa nams (Mentzendorff House)
Wander around the inside of this 17th-century house and discover how Riga's wealthy lived some 300 years ago. The building is filled with antique furniture, frescoes and household items. ⓐ Grēcinieku iela 18 ⓣ 67 21 29 51 ⓛ 11.00–17.00, closed Mon &Tues. Admission charge

Pulvertornis un Kara muzejs (Powder Tower & Latvian War Museum)
One of the city towers that helped to form the city's walled fortifications, the Pulvertornis dates back to 1330. Rebuilt several times, it took on its present identity in the 17th century because gunpowder came to be stored here. A military museum was added in 1919, with new structures attached in 1937 and 1939.
ⓐ Smilšu iela 20 ⓣ 67 22 81 47 ⓦ www.karamuzejs.lv

Rātslaukums (Town Hall Square) & Statue of Roland
In the 14th century statues of Roland began appearing all over northern Germany as a symbol of justice and freedom. He was considered to

DID YOU KNOW?
Most steeples of Riga churches are topped by gilded cockerels.
Contrary to the sinister biblical significance of this animal, in
Latvian folklore it stands for vigilance and safeguards from
evil. When the cock crows for the third time, the devil must
retreat back to hell. This practice of placing a cockerel on the
spire of a church dates from the Middle Ages, when it also had
a practical use as a weather vane.

be a just judge and defender of the accused, and so his statue was
placed in the Town Hall Square in front of the Guilds of Hanseatic
cities. The point of Roland's sword was the spot from which distances
were measured in Riga and Latvia.

Rīgas pils (Riga Castle)

Built in 1330, the Castle was originally constructed for the Grand
Master of the Livonian Order. It is now the official office of the Latvian
president who should take into account its bloody history. An angry
mob of townspeople ransacked the castle in response to the policies
of the hated Livonian Order. The complex also contains the Foreign
Art Museum and the Latvian History Museum. ⓐ Pils laukums 3

Rīgas vēstures un kuģniecības muzejs
(Riga's History and Navigation Museum)

This museum leads you through the process of how a small
settlement on the bank of the Rīdzene River grew into a large
Hanseatic city. A good, but sometimes ghoulish, collection that
includes a mummified hand and a 16th-century executioner's sword.

🔺 *These Three Brothers were born centuries apart*

ⓐ Palasta iela 4 ⓣ 67 21 13 58 ⓛ 10.00–17.00, closed Mon & Tues.
Admission charge

Svētā Pētera baznīca (St Peter's Church)

This 13th-century church was ruined during World War II and repaired
during the Soviet occupation. A 360° platform around the spire allows
you to view all of Riga and the Old Town – a perfect way to get your
bearings and plan your sightseeing.ⓐ Skārņu iela 19 ⓣ 67 22 94 26
ⓛ 10.00–18.00, closed Mon. Admission charge

Trīs brāļi (The Three Brothers)

Excellent examples of medieval dwellings. Number 17, built in the
1500s, is the oldest stone residential building in Latvia. Number 19
houses an architectural museum and number 21 took on its current
appearance in the 17th century. Viewed together they constitute
almost a textbook of the architectural development of Riga over the
centuries.ⓐ Mazā Pils iela 17, 19, 21 ⓛ 10.00–18.00, closed Sat & Sun

Zviedru vārti (The Swedish Gate)

The last remaining gate of the old city wall, built during the Swedish
reign. Legend has it that the city's medieval executioner once lived
above the gate and used to leave a red rose on the windowsill the
day someone was going to lose his head. The lion face was the
Swedish king's imperial symbol. ⓐ Corner of Torņa iela & Aldaru iela

CULTURE

The heart of the Old Town is Doma Laukums (Dome Square) where,
in summer, tables and chairs spill out into the area from cafés and
bars, creating a fun-filled atmosphere. And when the weather is less

cooperative for outdoor festivities folks flock to the interiors of the Opera House, live theatres and restaurants.

Carpe Diem

Go for the delicious international cuisine and stay for the music. Every evening jazz acts perform for the dinner crowd from around 19.00. ⓐ Meistaru iela 10/12 ⓣ 67 22 84 88

Forum Cinemas

With 14 screens, this is the second-largest cinema complex in Northern Europe. A bar and café make for a complete evening out. ⓐ 13 janvāra iela 8 ⓦ www.forumcinemas.lv

Kaļķu vārti

Although the ground floor is occupied by an upmarket restaurant, the cellar club often hosts concerts by local stars such as Eurovision superstar Marie N. ⓐ Kaļķu iela 11a ⓣ 67 21 25 75 ⓦ www.kalkuvarti.lv

Latvian National Opera

A magnificent concert hall originally intended to house the City of Riga's German Theatre, was completely renovated in 1995. State-of-the-art technology complements the pristine museum interior of 1862. The opera features world-famous stars as well as rising young talents. ⓐ Aspazijas bulvāris 3 ⓣ 67 07 37 77 ⓕ 67 22 89 30 ⓦ www.opera.lv

Latvian National Theatre

A resident company of about 40 actors is devoted to the presentation of Latvian classical plays and the development of original dramas by Latvian playwrights. ⓐ Kronvalda bulvāris 2 ⓣ 67 00 63 37

UNDER THE CLOCK

An excellent meeting place is the rectangular clock, advertising Laima Chocolate, on the eastern edge of the Old Town next to the Freedom Monument, where Brīvības iela and Aspazijas bulvāris intersect. Originally built in the 1920s so the masses wouldn't have an excuse to be late for work, it has been the starting point of many a sweet romance.

Vāgnera zāle (Wagner Hall)

Named after its most illustrious conductor, Richard Wagner, this small concert hall often hosts classical music concerts. ⓐ Vāgnera iela 4 ⓣ 67 22 71 05

RETAIL THERAPY

Emihls Gustavs Chocolate Although it has now become a chain of chocolate shops found in nearly every shopping centre, you can watch them make the sinfully delicious sweets by hand at this location. ⓐ Aspazijas bulvāris 24 ⓣ 67 22 83 33 ⓦ www.sokolade.lv

Galerija Centrs The old Latvian universal shopping centre of the 1930s has been completely changed and expanded and now comprises nearly an entire city block in Old Riga. Although UNESCO threatened to revoke the city's prestigious status as a world heritage site due to its construction, most locals are happy to have four floors of shops, cafés, a supermarket and even a day spa in the centre of town. ⓐ Audēju iela 16 ⓣ 67 01 80 18 ⓦ www.galerijacentrs.lv

Galerija Tornis A husband and wife team sells a wide variety of Latvian jewellery based on ancient Baltic designs found at archaeological sites around the country. Both Hillary Clinton and the queen of Denmark have shopped here. ⓐ Grēcinieku iela 11 (entrance from Pēterbaznīcas) ⓣ 67 22 02 70 ⓦ www.balturotas.lv

Globuss A decent selection of English-language books can be found within this shop, along with a second-floor café where you can relax and read English-language newspapers. ⓐ Vaļņu iela 26 ⓣ 67 22 69 57

Laima Did someone say chocolate? This Old Town location is just one of many places in Riga to get your sugar hit. Laima Chocolate is truly good stuff. Available at several locations around Riga. ⓐ Smilšu iela 8 ⓦ www.laima.lv

Skārņu iela, Vaļņu iela and Līvu laukums You'll find people hawking anything from knitwear, amber and artwork at these locations – however, *caveat emptor* (buyer beware).

Tīne This is where you can find, well, practically any kind of souvenir you might desire. Spread over two floors is a wide selection of ceramics, amber, trinkets, linen, wool mittens and socks. ⓐ Vaļņu iela 2 ⓣ 67 21 67 28

Upe Owned by a popular local folk singer Ainars Mielavs, 'River' is a great place to buy Latvian music from traditional lullabies to modern rock. It also sells Latvian instruments, wooden toys and other handmade souvenirs. ⓐ Vāgnera iela 5 ⓣ 67 22 61 19 ⓦ www.upett.lv

Valters un Rapa Large bookshop, well-stocked with coffee-table books about Riga, along with stationery and calendars.
ⓐ Aspazijas bulvāris 24 ❶ 67 22 74 82 ⓦ www.valtersunrapa.lv

TAKING A BREAK

Alus Sēta £ ❶ One of a number of Latvian restaurants owned by the Lido chain, 'The Beer Garden' is a kitschy collection of local memorabilia, wooden tables and assorted rustic décor. Take a tray and choose from a wide variety of creamy salads and cholesterol-laden meat and potato dishes. It also offers its own micro-brewed beer on draught. ⓐ Tirgoņu iela 6 ❶ 67 22 24 31 ⓦ www.lido.lv
🕒 11.00–24.00

🔺 For hearty Latvian food and a tasty brew head to Alus Sēta

Picnix £ ❷ This European-style sandwich shop is so small it offers discounts for takeaway. Enjoy delicious salads, panini and or a 'picnix' which is a wide variety of fresh ingredients like tandoori marinated chicken with mozzarella, avocado, sun-dried tomatoes and pesto on its own homemade bread. Outside seating is available in summer. ➊ Aldaru 11/6 ☎ 67 22 56 07 ⏰ 08.00–20.00, closed Sat & Sun

Rozengrāls £ ❸ Located in what used to be the Town Hall's private wine cellar in ancient times, this theme restaurant offers waiting staff in period costume and dishes based on medieval recipes. No potatoes or tomatoes are listed on the menu because they weren't available in Riga in the 1400s. Thankfully, you can order local beer as well as honey mead. ➊ Rozena iela 1 ☎ 67 22 03 56 ⊕ www.rozengrals.lv ⏰ 12.00–24.00

Soraksans £ ❹ Staff in traditional Korean outfits overwhelm patrons with their friendliness and offer help navigating the unique menu of tongue-twisting dishes served on sizzling iron pans or in ceramic pots. The *kimchi* is guaranteed to have you reaching for your water glass and *bibimpab* will keep you coming back for more. ➊ Miesnieku iela 12 ☎ 67 22 90 68 ⊕ www.soraksans.lv ⏰ 12.00–23.00

Melnie Mūki ££ ❺ Although reservations are recommended in the evening, you can usually get a table here during the day. An extensive menu of international and fusion cuisine, friendly service and romantic ambience make the 'Black Monks' a local favourite for those who appreciate refined food and drink. ➊ Jāṇa Sēta 1 (entrance from Kalēju) ☎ 67 21 50 06 ⏰ 12.00–24.00

AFTER DARK

RESTAURANTS

Melnais Kaķis £–££ ❻ The 'Black Cat' is the place to go for food, billiards, video games as well as beer and alcohol when most other bars have closed their doors. ⓐ Meistaru iela 10/12 ❶ 67 21 10 21 ⓦ www.kakis.lv ⓛ 08.00–07.00

Dickens ££ ❼ A favourite for visiting Brits, this authentic English pub offers a wide variety of foreign and domestic beer including hand-pumped ales from London. You can watch Sky Sports on TV, eat a full English breakfast or just have a chat with the person next to you in your native tongue. ⓐ Grēcinieku iela 9/1 ❶ 67 21 3087 ⓦ www.dickens.lv ⓛ 11.00–01.00

Lounge 8 ££ ❽ Riga's hippest cocktail bar offers dozens of tables surrounding a central bar, tasty international cuisine, a walk-in humidor and a giant smoking lounge behind a glass wall at the far end. You can reserve a table on its website. ⓐ Vaļņu iela 19 ❶ 67 35 95 95 ⓦ www.lounge8.lv ⓛ 12.00–24.00 Sun–Wed, 12.00–03.00 Thur–Sat

Bon Vivant ££–£££ ❾ Riga's only Belgian bar offers Benelux decorations, an authentic menu of delicious dishes like mussels, sausages and pommes frites, not to mention a fantastic selection of draught beers served in their proper glasses. ⓐ Mārstaļu iela 8 ❶ 67 22 65 85 ⓦ www.bon-vivant.lv ⓛ 11.00–01.00

Nobu ££–£££ ❿ Part cocktail lounge, part upmarket Japanese restaurant, you'll be hard-pressed to find a trendier place to have

a martini and sushi at the same time. 🅐 Grēcinieku iela 28
🕿 67 35 97 46 🕓 12.00–24.00 Sun–Thur, 12.00–02.00 Fri & Sat

BARS & CLUBS

Četri Balti Krekli Named after a classic local film, this is the
best place in the city to see Latvian acts perform at the weekend.
Bouncers, however, will prohibit entry to anyone wearing trainers
so put on your dancing shoes. 🅐 Vecpilsētas iela 12 🕿 67 21 38 85
🅦 www.krekli.lv 🕓 20.00–04.00

Cuba Café Assorted Caribbean decorations as well as some photos
of Castro and Guevara adorn the walls of this popular cocktail bar
just off of Dome Square. Although beer is also available, don't pass up
what may be the best mojitos in town. 🅐 Jaun iela 15 🕿 67 22 43 62
🕓 12.00–02.00 Sun–Thur, 12.00–04.00 Fri & Sat

NB Pool and snooker tables for as far the eye can see on two floors
open 24 hours a day. Although it doesn't offer a menu beyond peanuts
and crisps, it does have plenty of drinks. 🅐 Šķūņu iela 9 🕿 67 22 63 51
🕓 24 hours

Paddy Whelan's If you're hungry you might consider another bar,
but if it's beer and sports you're after, then look no further. Flat
screen TVs showing Sky Sports adorn the walls and hang from the
ceilings and over 20 different brews are on draught. 🅐 Grēcinieku iela
4 🕿 67 21 01 50 🕓 11.00–01.00 Sun–Thur, 11.00–03.00 Fri & Sat

Pulkvedim neviens neraksta Also known simply as Pulkvedis or the
Colonel, it's hit or miss with this club. One night it's full of British
tourists dancing to Michael Jackson and the next, with bohemian

Latvians listening to alternative rock. Don't miss the cocktail lounge downstairs with pink shag carpeting on the walls and the floral designs à la Austin Powers. ❸ Peldu iela 26/28 ❶ 67 21 38 86 ❿ www.pulkvedis.lv ⏱ 20.00–03.00 Mon–Thur, 20.00–05.00 Fri & Sat, closed Sun

Rīgas Balzams Not surprisingly, this cosy, candle-lit bar specialises in the Latvian national drink, Riga Black Balsam. Drink it neat, in your coffee, with blackcurrant juice or, if you're not afraid of the morning after, with local sparkling wine. ❸ Torņa iela 4 (Jēkaba Kazarmas) ❶ 67 21 44 94 ⏱ 11.00–24.00

● *Paddy Whelan's provides a taste of Ireland in Riga*

City Centre

East of the tangled streets of Old Riga rises New Riga, the two areas well defined by the city's old defensive moat, the Pilsētas kanāls (see page 64) or City Canal. Wide boulevards and park areas mark the 19th-century influence, and the abundant art nouveau architecture adds the flavour of the wealthy early 20th century.

This part of Riga is filled with monuments and memorials to the recent turmoil that have affected this country. On Brīvības bulvāris stands the Freedom Monument, affectionately known as 'Milda', a striking liberty figure, crowned with three stars. This monument became a rallying point of the Latvian Independence movement in 1987. During the years of Soviet occupation a statue of Lenin, facing in the opposite direction, was erected only two blocks east of the monument. It has since been removed.

North of the Freedom Monument, red stone slabs stand as memorials to the dead of 20 January 1991, when Soviet troops stormed the Ministry of the Interior at nearby Raiņa bulvāris 6. This site is known as the Bastion Hill Memorial.

The impressive National Museum of Art lies at the northern end of the Esplanade Park. The permanent collection features works of Latvian artists, and other artists are featured in temporary or travelling exhibitions. Once a planetarium during the Soviet occupation the Russian Orthodox Cathedral, at the southern end of the Esplanade, has returned to its status as a church. In the same park you will also find a monument to Jānis Rainis, Latvia's national poet, who some say would have been world-famous had he written his works in a less obscure language.

● *The Freedom Monument – Milda is Riga's lady liberty*

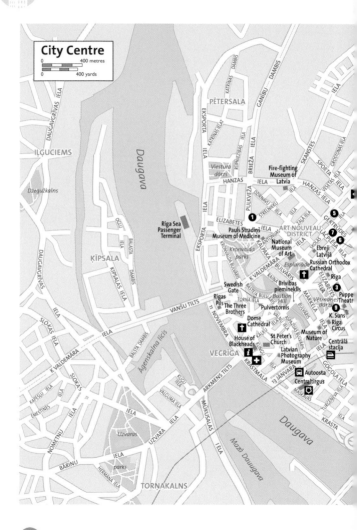

City Centre

0 _____ 400 metres
0 _____ 400 yards

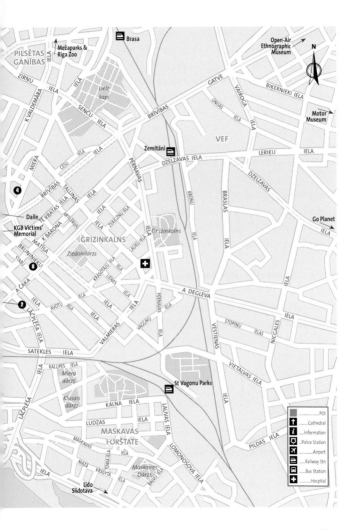

Most of suburban Riga is not much to write home about. Like all good urban sprawl, it's a mix of the good, the bad and the strip mall. One outstanding exception is Mežaparks (Forest Park). This area was once Riga's poshest residential district. Most of the construction took place prior to World War I and continued until the 1930s, and it includes examples of art nouveau, Romanticism and Rationalism.

SIGHTS & ATTRACTIONS

Bastejkalns (Bastion Hill)
Five memorial stones in this central location are a haunting reminder of the Soviet crackdown in Riga in 1991. Five citizens were killed as Soviet troops stormed a nearby Interior Ministry building.

Brīvības piemineklis (Freedom Monument)
This national shrine was unveiled in 1935. Designed by Kārlis Zāle, the friezes around the base of the structure depict Latvians singing, working and fighting for their freedom. The three stars in the woman's crown depict the three historical regions of the country – Kurzeme, Vidzeme and Latgale. It is a tradition to place flowers at the base of the monument. During the Soviet occupation this act could mean a quick trip to Siberia. The Honour Guard changes every hour on the hour from 09.00–18.00. ❸ Brīvības bulvāris & Raiņa bulvāris

Art nouveau district
The increasing prosperity of the late 19th century and early 20th century resulted in an expansion of Riga beyond its central hub. This could not have happened at a more fortuitous time of design than that of the explosion of the art nouveau style.

⬥ The Guards of the Motherland stare out from the Freedom Monument

The architectural style that developed in Austria and Germany, where it was known as *Jugendstil*, has left its imprint on cities from Paris to St Petersburg. Buildings are characterised by their decorations: floral patterns, human faces and mythical figures. This was more than just a fashion trend: art nouveau infiltrated almost all aspects of life at that time. Evidence of its influence could be found on everything from buildings to tableware, paintings to cocktail shakers. At the time this style was becoming popular, Riga was a very important port in the Russian empire, with a booming economy, growing population and lots of money to spend. The result was such that nearly 40 per cent of the buildings in Riga's city centre have been designed in the style of art nouveau.

Most of Riga's art nouveau treasures escaped the devastation of World War II and the majority of buildings remained mainly untouched. Naturally, the stagnation of the Soviet era had a devastating effect on these unique architectural monuments. Beautiful apartments that once housed only one family were divided up among groups of over 20 people who shared a single kitchen and toilet. However, property nationalised by the Communists was returned to pre-1940 owners spurring an economic boom.

Take a walking tour of the best of the art nouveau buildings. Start at the north corner of the Esplanade and go west on Elizabetes iela. You will see many buildings designed by Mikhail Eisenstein, father of the famous Russian filmmaker, Sergei Eisenstein, who directed the classic *Battleship Potemkin*. Continue along Elizabetes, turn right on Strēlnieku iela and then turn right again on Alberta iela. Nymphs and mythical figures grace the façades of everyday buildings. Floral motifs bloom on the fronts of apartment buildings and bay windows

⏵ *In Riga you can see art nouveau at its most theatrical*

sprout like weeds. No wonder the utilitarian architecture of the Soviet era stands out in stark comparison. Note the plaque at Alberta iela 2 dedicated to renowned philosopher and essayist Sir Isaiah Berlin who spent his early childhood in the building. The first Jew to hold a fellowship at Oxford, his father was a successful timber merchant in Riga.

Centrāltirgus (Central Market)

At the end of its construction in 1930, Riga's Central Market was the largest and most modern marketplace in Europe. The market was built with five World War 1-era zeppelin hangars. Four of these buildings still function as meat, fish, produce and dairy markets. The atmosphere bustles with activity, and although you might find a few merchants open to haggling, the majority are reluctant to do so. ❷ Centrāltirgus iela, near the central railway station ⓦ www.centraltirgus.lv
🕑 08.00–17.00 Tues–Sat, 08.00–16.00 Sun & Mon

Dabas muzejs (Museum of Nature)

This museum of natural history is one of the oldest museums in the country, dating back to 1846. The collections, spread over four floors, include a variety of fossils, plants, animals and some interactive exhibits. ⓐ Barona iela 4 ⓣ 67 35 60 24 ⓦ www.dabasmuzejs.gov.lv ⓛ 10.00–17.00 Wed, Fri & Sat, 10.00–18.00 Thur, 10.00–16.00 Sun, closed Mon & Tues. Admission charge

Ebreji Latvijā (Jews in Latvia)

This small museum located in the Riga Jewish Association house chronicles the life of Jews in Latvia from medieval times to the present. It illustrates the contributions Jews made to Latvian society and how their communities were extinguished during the Holocaust. Visitors can also watch a film about Jewish life in Latvia. ⓐ Skolas iela 6 ⓣ 67 28 34 84 ⓛ 12.00–17.00, closed Fri & Sat.

● *The zeppelins have been replaced by stalls in Riga's central market*

KGB Victims' Memorial

The rusted portal on this neglected building that now houses a police station serves as a reminder of a terrible chapter in Latvian history. The text to its left sums it up: 'During the Soviet occupation the state security agency, the KGB, imprisoned, tortured, killed and morally humiliated its victims in this building.' ⓐ Brīvības iela 61 (viewed from Stabu)

Latvijas ugunsdzēsības muzejs (Fire-Fighting Museum of Latvia)

An art nouveau-style firehouse? Yes, indeed. This museum is housed in a former fire station built in that classic style. Inside you'll find collections featuring equipment, flags, uniforms and photographs outlining the history of fire-fighting from the 19th century until today. ⓐ Hanzas iela 5 ❶ 67 33 13 34 ❶ 11.00–17.00, closed Mon & Tues. Admission charge

Nacionālais mākslas muzejs (National Art Museum)

A fine and varied collection of Latvian art that includes the work of such Latvian old masters as Vilhelms Purvītis, Janis Rozentāls and Ludolfs Liberts. ⓐ Valdemāra iela 10a ❶ 67 32 44 61 ⓦ www.vmm.lv ❶ 11.00–17.00, closed Tues

P. Stradiņa medicīnas vēstures muzejs (Pauls Stradiņš Museum of Medicine)

Latvia's famous Dr Pauls Stradiņš collected antique, folk and unusual cures and medicines for more than 30 years. This collection has been assembled into one of the largest museums of medicine in the world. Quirky, and sometimes a little bit morbid, this museum will definitely intrigue. ⓐ Antonijas iela 1 ❶ 67 22 26 65 ⓦ www.mvm.lv ❶ 11.00–17.00 Fri–Wed, 11.00–19.00 Thur. Admission charge

FURTHER AFIELD

Latvijas etnogrāfiskais brīvdabas muzejs (Latvian Open-air Ethnographic Museum)

Over 100 hectares (240 acres) of life as it used to be during a more pastoral period in Latvia's history. Farmsteads, windmills, churches and fishing villages have been relocated to this site and restored for posterity. You can watch craftsmen ply their trades, see costumed 'villagers' and partake of Latvian food and drink in the tavern.
ⓐ Brīvības gatve 440 ⓣ 67 99 45 15 ⓦ www.virmus.lv ⓛ 10.00–17.00
ⓝ Bus: 1 to Brīvdabas muzejs. Admission charge

Mežaparks (Forest Park)

This area was once Riga's poshest residential district. Most of the construction took place prior to World War I and continued until the 1930s. Rent a boat on the lake or in-line skates at the entrance, visit the Song Festival grounds or try one of the children's attractions with the kids. ⓝ Tram: 11 to Mežaparks

Rīgas Motormuzejs (Riga Motor Museum)

You don't have to be a gear head or a youngster to appreciate the assembled collection of automobiles from bygone days. If you ever wondered what Stalin drove, or yearned to see the car Brezhnev crashed on a joy ride, this is the place. There is also an exhibit of antique motorbikes on site. ⓐ Eizenšteina iela 6 ⓣ 67 09 71 70
ⓦ www.motormuzejs.lv ⓛ 10.00–18.00. Admission charge

Rīgas zoodārzs (Riga Zoo)

Set amid the hilly pines of Mežaparks, the zoo has a substantial collection of animals, including zebras, camels and bears. The tropical

reptile house is its crowning jewel. ⓐ Meža Prospekts 1 ❶ 67 51 84 09
🕐 10.00–17.00. Admission charge Ⓝ Tram: 11 to Mežaparks

CULTURE

Daile
Older films are shown here at discounted rates. ⓐ Barona iela 31
❶ 67 28 38 54

Go Planet
A huge entertainment complex in the middle of the Soviet suburbs,
it offers billiards, bars, restaurants, laser tag, go-carts, virtual reality
games, a 3D cinema and children's attractions. ⓐ Gunāra Astras iela 2b
❶ 67 14 63 46 Ⓦ www.goplanet.lv Ⓝ Tram: 17 to Mēbeļu nams

K.Suns
A small theatre in the trendy Berga Bazārs shopping gallery shows
European and art house films from around the globe. ⓐ Elizabetes
iela 83/85 ❶ 67 28 54 11

Lido Slidotava (Lido Skating Rink)
The active life is certainly a part of Riga's culture, so strap on a pair
of in-line skates in summer or ice skates in winter and join the throng
at this huge outdoor rink. After you've worked up an appetite have
a snack or a beer before pressing on. ⓐ Krasta iela 76 ❶ 67 50 44 20
🕐 10.00–23.00 Ⓦ www.ac.lido.lv Ⓝ Bus: 17A to Lido

Leļļu teātris (Puppet Theatre)
You have to love a theatre that allows you to adjust the height of
your seat, so that even the smallest patron can get a good view of
the stage. ⓐ Barona iela 16/18 ❶ 67 28 54 18 Ⓦ www.puppet.lv

Rīga

Once called the Splendid Palace, the ornate old-world interior makes for a classic cinema experience. This is where Rigans head to see international films as well as Hollywood blockbusters. ⓐ Elizabetes iela 61 ⓣ 67 28 11 05 ⓦ www.cinema-riga.lv

Rīgas Cirks (Riga Circus)

At nearly a century old, the Riga Circus is the only permanent circus in the Baltics. The shows run from mid-October until April, with special productions during both Christmas and Easter. Not your usual circus, and not to everyone's taste, the acts include some performing pigs and not-so-performing cats. ⓐ Merķeļa iela 4 ⓣ 67 21 32 79 ⓦ www.cirks.lv

RETAIL THERAPY

Alfa Possibly Latvia's largest shopping centre. Hundreds of shops are at your disposal as well as a food court and a Rimi hypermarket. ⓐ Brīvības gatve 372 ⓦ www.alfaparks.lv ⓛ 10.00–22.00 ⓝ Tram: 6 to Alfa

Antikvariāts Del Arte This small antique shop sells ceramics, paintings, books and a wide variety of Latvian memorabilia. ⓐ Barona iela 16/18 ⓣ 29 48 15 68 ⓛ 11.00–19.00 Mon–Fri, 11.00–16.00 Sat, closed Sun

Art Nouveau Riga Why buy amber and sweaters when you can purchase a souvenir that is truly indicative of Riga? Plaster faces based on 19th-century artwork that adorns façades of local buildings and a wide variety of mugs, books, postcards and even clothing based on art nouveau design are all available here. ⓐ Strēlnieku iela 9 ⓣ 67 33 30 30 ⓦ www.artnouveauriga.lv ⓛ 08.00–19.00

Barona Centrs A small shopping centre, smack in the middle of town.
ⓐ Barona iela 46 ⓣ 67 50 84 00 ⓦ www.baronacentrs.lv
ⓛ 10.00–21.00 Mon–Sat, 10.00–18.00 Sun

Jāņa Sēta The best map shop in the Baltics also sells a wide variety
of guides to Latvia and hundreds of destinations around the globe.
ⓐ Elizabetes 83/85 ⓣ 67 24 08 94 ⓦ www.mapshop.lv ⓛ 10.00–19.00
Mon–Fri, 10.00–17.00 Sat, closed Sun

Origo Great big shopping centre in and around the train station filled
with everything, including fashion outlets and services such as dry
cleaning. ⓐ Stacijas laukums 2 ⓦ www.origo.lv ⓛ 10.00–22.00

Senā klēts The 'Ancient Barn' is the only shop in Riga to specialise
in Latvian folk costumes. It also sells jewellery, traditional blankets
and other handmade crafts. ⓐ Merķeļa iela 13 ⓣ 67 24 23 98
ⓛ 10.00–18.00 Mon–Fri, 10.00–17.00 Sat, closed Sun

Stockmann Finland's number one department store offers four
floors of fashion for everyone and everything in your home. And,
if that's not enough, it also boasts the best supermarket in Riga with
hard-to-get items not available anywhere else. ⓐ 13 janvāra iela 8
ⓦ www.stockmann.lv ⓛ 09.00–22.00

Vidzemes tirgus (Vidzeme Market) Similar to the Central Market
but on a much smaller scale. ⓐ Brīvības iela 90 ⓣ 67 31 17 96
ⓦ www.vidzemestirgus.lv

Ziedu tirgus (Flower Market) An amazing array of flowers for a whole
city block. ⓐ Tērbatas between Merķeļa and Elizabetes ⓛ 24hrs

TAKING A BREAK

Ai Karamba £ ❶ Riga's best breakfast destination is designed to look like an American-style diner, complete with a long counter flanked with barstools on one side. Order fried egg, a burger or a steak at any time of the day, take advantage of its excellent beer and cocktail selection. ⓐ Pulkveža Brieža iela 2 ❶ 67 33 46 72 ⓦ www.aikaramba.lv ⓛ 08.00–24.00 Tues–Sat, 10.00–24.00 Sun

Charlestons £ ❷ This trendy restaurant provides its patrons with a warm atmosphere, excellent service, outstanding international cuisine and a fantastic summer courtyard terrace. Its cappuccino bar opens early. ⓐ Blaumaņa iela 38/40 ❶ 67 77 05 72 ⓦ www.charlestons.lv ⓛ 12.00–24.00

Vairāk Saules £–££ ❸ This family-style restaurant has an impressive selection of international dishes as well as over 20 different pizzas. It also offers a kids' menu and play area. ⓐ Dzirnavu iela 60 ❶ 67 28 28 78 ⓦ www.vairaksaules.lv ⓛ 09.00–23.00

Aragats ££ ❹ Family owned and operated, this Armenian restaurant has the friendliest staff in town. Don't miss the sand-boiled coffee or Stalin's favourite wine. ⓐ Miera iela 15 ❶ 67 37 34 45 ⓛ 13.00–22.00 Mon–Sat

AFTER DARK

RESTAURANTS
5 Vilki £ ❺ Five Wolves is owned by a member of a local motorcycle club called the Wind Brothers Order. You can eat breakfast food,

chicken wings or a pork chop here, shoot darts or do as the bikers dressed in leather do and drink a Tērvetes brew. You can also order vodka by the bottle presented in a block of ice. ⓐ Stabu iela 6 ⓣ 67 29 95 55 ⓛ 10.00–24.00

Habibi ££ ⓺ This Middle Eastern-style café offers a space completely covered in oriental carpets, dozens of different tobaccos to smoke in *hookahs*, and food and drink as well as belly dancers at the weekend. ⓐ Ģertrūdes iela 14 ⓣ 67 29 01 55 ⓛ 13.00–24.00

⬥ *In addition to great views the Skyline Bar also offers a sense of style*

Pie Kristapa Kunga ££ ❼ Enjoy Latvian, Russian, European or Middle Eastern food in this restaurant designed to look like a Crusader castle. The beer selection is impressive, you can smoke hookahs in the cellar or choose your dinner from a tiny trout pond. ⓐ Baznīcas iela 27/29 ❶ 67 29 48 99 ⓦ www.piekristapakunga.lv ⓛ 11.00–23.00

Staburags ££ ❽ There is no better place to have a Latvian meal with table service. A maze of rustic niches on two floors serves as the perfect backdrop for a meal of pork knuckle, potatoes and sauerkraut. Do as Romano Prodi or Helmut Kohl did when they dined here and order a mug of Užavas beer. ⓐ A Čaka iela 55 ❶ 67 29 97 87 ⓦ www.lido.lv ⓛ 12.00–24.00

Hotel Bergs Restaurant £££ ❾ Stylish, expensive and unforgettable, its chefs frequently create a new menu to reflect the season of the year. Order anything from scallops to duck as you admire the view from Riga's premier design hotel. ⓐ Elizabetes iela 83/85 ❶ 67 77 09 57 ⓦ www.hotelbergs.lv ⓛ 12.00–24.00 Mon–Sat

BARS & CLUBS
Club Essential Riga's most popular techno, house and hip-hop club regularly imports famous DJs from around Europe to keep the beautiful people coming back. A cinema in former days, it has plenty of space to support the crowds of people queued up outside its doors at the weekend. ⓐ Skolas iela 2 ❶ 67 24 22 89 ⓦ www.essential.lv ⓛ 22.00–06.00 Thur–Sun. Admission charge

Klondaika The 'Klondike' looks like the set of Spaghetti Western, but with a better selection of whiskey. Although it's also a popular place to eat pseudo Tex-Mex food, it's one of the few pubs in the area that's open until the wee hours of the morning. It also offers slot machines and pool tables. **ⓐ** Dzirnavu iela 59 **ⓣ** 67 24 03 66 **ⓦ** www.klondaika.lv **ⓛ** 09.00–07.00

Red Fred This could be the only bar in Eastern Europe with a fire-fighting theme. Although the grilled food is pricey, the dozens of draught beers on offer are surprisingly inexpensive, so skip the steak and order a Czech Budweiser. **ⓐ** Dzirnavu iela 62 **ⓣ** 67 36 51 13 **ⓛ** 12.00–24.00

La Rocca Although teenagers and twenty-somethings come for the techno, the clientele and the cheap cocktails, La Rocca also offers a casino, a strip club and an exclusive bathhouse for more mature guests in a different tax bracket. **ⓐ** Brīvības iela 96 **ⓣ** 67 50 60 30 **ⓦ** www.larocca.lv **ⓛ** 22.00–07.00 Thur–Sun. Admission charge

Skyline Bar You really haven't been to Riga unless you've had a drink at the funky cocktail bar on the 26th floor of the Reval Hotel Latvija. The views are unparalleled and the interior is trendy, so you probably won't even mind the glacially slow service. **ⓐ** Elizabetes iela 55 **ⓣ** 67 77 22 22 **ⓦ** www.revalhotels.com **ⓛ** 15.00–02.00

Stella Pub Although it serves plenty of Benelux beer from Stella Artois to Hoegaarden, it actually fancies itself a sports bar. The walls are covered with photos of local athletes and the short bartender with the grey hair is a famous former marathon runner. In short, it's a good place to watch football and drink beer. **ⓐ** Lāčplēša iela 35 **ⓣ** 67 28 35 12 **ⓦ** www.stellapub.lv **ⓛ** 10.00–24.00 Mon–Sat, 14.00–22.00 Sun

---

● *Sigulda's public buildings and parks make it a popular daytrip destination*

Northern Latvia

A day trip east of Riga will introduce you to some of the loveliest parts of Latvia. If you've had all you want of the medieval architecture, hustle and bustle of city life in Riga then it must be time to grab a train and head for the outdoors life. Be sure to have extra cards for your digital camera because you're going to use a lot of pixels in this part of the country.

The valley of the Gauja River, between the towns of Valmiera and Sigulda, is possibly the most picturesque area of Latvia. It is also one of the most historic. The river has cut its winding path through the sandstone, leaving rocky cliffs and forested banks.

In 1207, about the same time as Riga was being founded, the area was split between the Knights of the Sword (later the Livonian Order – a German crusading order allied to the Teutonic Knights) who got the south bank of the river, and the Archbishop of Riga, who claimed the north bank. The area remained split between various invading factions for centuries. Naturally, the indigenous Livs, close cousins if the Estonians, had no say in the matter. Although the rolling, forested hills in the area are barely 100 m (330 ft) high, for over a century the town of Sigulda and its picturesque surroundings have been known as Latvia's Switzerland.

Starting at Sigulda, only 50 km (31 miles) east of Riga, this destination is easily reached by train, bus or car. It's a part of the scenic Gauja National Park. Besides many caves, hiking trails and nature paths, the area is covered with castles, palaces and churches. The park is perfect for canoeing, hiking and just kicking back.

Cēsis, a short 90 km (56 miles) from Riga, is easily reached by car, train or bus. There is an hourly bus service between Riga and Cēsis, and four trains a day, also stopping at Sigulda. All the sights of the

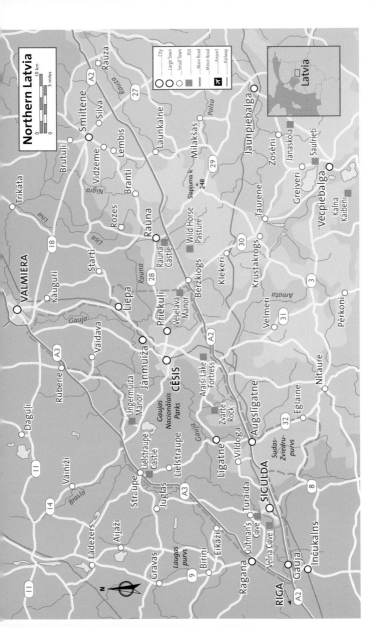

town centre are within a short distance of each other, making for a compact sightseeing experience.

SIGULDA

Sigulda is the closest entry point to the area. Following the restoration of Latvia's independence, Sigulda experienced a resurgence in the preservation of public buildings and parks, and, more importantly, in the services offered to tourists. Sigulda is also the site of the Latvian bobsleigh run (see below and page 110). In the spring a town festival is held around the time of the cherry trees blossoming, in summer an open-air Opera Festival takes place in the castle ruins, autumn is the time to watch the glorious colours of the trees, while winter is the season for skiing and bobsleigh racing.

GETTING THERE
Sigulda is accessible by both bus and train. The trip with either mode of transport should take a little over an hour and a return ticket should cost roughly 3Ls. You can also rent a car and drive there. Take Brīvības iela north from Riga and follow signs for Sigulda.

SIGHTS & ATTRACTIONS
Bobsleja trase (Bobsleigh Track)
The giant run of the national bobsleigh track was built by Yugoslavian experts in 1981. To get there, walk a few hundred metres from the station along the train tracks in the direction of Riga. You won't be able to miss it (see page 110). ❸ Šveices iela 13 ❶ 67 97 38 13 Ⓦ www.lgk.lv

Dainu Kaļns (Folk Song Hill)
Stroll among giant stone sculpture on Folk Song Hill. The statues

⬤ *Anyone can try out the exhilarating sport of bobsleigh*

reflect the various characters and aspects of Latvian folklore.
ⓐ next to Turaida Castle

Gaisa trošu ceļš – Vagoniņš (Gauja Valley Cable Car)

Take in the gorgeous Gauja Valley and the Turaida Castle from a cable car as it crosses from one side of the river to the other. The Krimulda Castle ruins are directly to your right when you step out on the north side of the river. After hours, it's used for bungee jumping. ⓐ Poruka iela 14 ① 67 97 25 31 ⓦ www.lgk.lv ① 10.00–19.30. Admission charge

Gūtmaņa ala (Gutman's Cave)

Measuring 19.8 m deep, 12 m wide and 10 m high (64 x 40 x 33 ft), this is the largest natural cave in the Baltics. If you look closely, you can see hundreds of inscriptions in its sandstone walls, some dating back to the 18th century. ⓐ 50m (150 ft) off Turaidas iela

Krimuldas pils (Krimulda Manor)

This yellow neo-classical building was once the seat of an aristocratic German family, but it now serves as a sanatorium and is closed to the public. However, the grounds are open, and worth a visit. Nearby are the ruins of Krimulda Castle. Built in the 13th century, it overlooks the valley. ⓐ Mednieku iela 3 ① 67 97 22 32 ⓦ www.krimuldaspils.lv

Pēterala (Peter's Cave)

This is a narrow cave in a sandstone wall along the embankment of the Vejupe river. The cave is only 6.5 m (20 ft) long and 5.3 m (17 ft) high. The story of the cave is that, during Swedish rule in the 17th century, a farmer named Peter hid in the cave in order to escape being drafted

● *The dramatic entrance to Gutman's cave, the largest in the Baltics*

into the army. Another legend claims that a local clergyman hid here and christened several children. Today, there is a path from Pēteralas iela and convenient steps leading to the cave for your exploration.

Siguldas pils un pilsdrupas (Sigulda Castle and castle ruins)

Once a mighty fortification built by German crusaders in the first decades of the 13th century, it was sacked during the Great Northern War (1700–1721) and was never rebuilt. The sturdy rock walls of the chapel are still in good repair after many centuries of neglect but all that remains of the castle is the impressive gate. A small amphitheatre was built on the grounds which hosts a variety of concerts in summer. Before you reach the ruins you'll notice the 19th-century New Castle, an impressive manor house that serves as the seat of government for the town. An upmarket restaurant with views of the ruins is also available inside. ⓐ Pils 16 and 18

Turaidas pils (Turaida Castle)

Sigulda's most impressive architectural wonder is perched on a hill overlooking the Gauja River Valley. Although its 13th-century splendour has been lovingly restored for many years, the shiny, new red bricks are a bit of a disappointment when viewed up close. It's best viewed from the Sigulda cable car where your imagination can run wild. Inside is a museum and a gift shop and you can also climb to the top of the tower for excellent views. The museum complex also includes one of the oldest wooden churches in Latvia as well as a sculpture park and the grave of the Rose of Turaida. ⓐ Turaidas iela 10 ⓣ 67 97 14 02 ⓦ www.turaidas-muzejs.lv ⓛ 10.00–18.00 May–Sept, 10.00–17.00 Oct–Apr. Admission charge

---

● *No trip to Sigulda is complete without a stop at Turaida Castle*

THE ROSE OF TURAIDA

In 1601, a fierce battle took place at Turaida Castle. Legend has it that afterward a scribe searched the battlefield for anyone who might have survived and came across a baby girl, still in the arms of its dead mother. The scribe called her Maija and raised her in the castle as if she were his own child. When she came of age she fell in love with a local commoner who planned to marry her. Unfortunately, a jealous soldier wanted her for himself, but she refused his advances. He later tricked her into meeting him at Gutman's Cave where he tried to have his way with her. Although there are many different stories about her final hours, it is generally believed that the soldier killed her there and then. Now, newlyweds place flowers on her grave as a tribute to the power of love. Look for her final resting place under a gnarled linden tree near the entrance to the park.

ACTIVE LIFE

Aerodium The only vertical wind tunnel in Eastern Europe simulates the feeling of skydiving freefall and is guaranteed to get your adrenaline pumping. ⓐ A2 Riga – Sigulda highway ⓣ 28 38 44 00 ⓦ www.aerodium.lv ⓛ 18.00–20.00 Tue–Fri, 12.00–20.00 Sat & Sun

Bobsleigh track Be bold! Take a ride on the giant run. Although speeds during competitions can reach 125 kmh (78 mph), your trip will be toned down a little. ⓐ Šveices iela 13, Sigulda ⓣ 67 97 38 13 ⓛ 12.00–17.00 Sat & Sun

Bungee jumping Can't get enough fear? Try the bungee jump from a cable car at a height of 43 m (142 ft) over the Gauja River. ⓐ Poruka iela 14, Sigulda ⓣ 26 44 06 60 ⓦ www.lgk.lv ⓛ from 18.30 Fri–Sun, May–Oct

Hot air balloon rides Gently drift over the scenic Gauja Valley and the towns of Cēsis and Sigulda. ⓐ Mūkusalas iela 41, Riga ⓣ 67 61 16 14 ⓦ www.altius.lv

Off-road go-carts Rent off-road mini-buggies and take a cruise over a private parcel of land in the countryside. Bumpy, fun and good for the motorheads among you. ⓐ 300 m beyond Sigulda on the Vidzeme Highway ⓣ 26 77 78 80 ⓦ www.crazycars.lv

Reiņa trase Six trails, a snowboard park, a pond for ice-skating, a cross-country skiing track, snow tubing and five lifts await you only a stone's throw from Sigulda. ⓐ Kalnzaķi, Krimuldas pagasts ⓣ 29 14 89 89 ⓦ www.reinatrase.lv

Turaidas Staļļi A more gentle activity with a pony ride or a horse ride with an instructor's supervision. ⓐ Turaidas 10, Sigulda ⓣ 29 26 84 57

Water sports Makars Tourism Agency rents rafts, canoes and rowboats to explore the River Gauja. A camping area is also available. ⓐ Peldu iela 2, Sigulda ⓣ 29 24 49 48 ⓦ www.makars.lv

RETAIL THERAPY

Galerija Tornis Located in the observation tower of Turaida Castle, this shop sells jewellery based on ancient Baltic designs found at archaeological digs throughout the country. ⓐ Turaidas iela 10, Sigulda ⓣ 67 97 13 73 ⓛ 11.00–18.00 May–Oct, closed Sun

TAKING A BREAK

Kaķu Māja (Cat House) £ Cosy little bistro and bar serving a good selection of Latvian staples and some salad selections for those seeking healthier fare. The beer selection is modest, the interior rustic, and the aromas from the adjoining bakery are tempting. ⓐ Pils iela 8, Sigulda ⓣ 29 15 01 01 ⓦ www.cathouse.lv ⓛ 08.00–23.00

Trīs Draugi £ A budget traveller's buffet dream. Good and cheap food such as grilled meat, beef stroganoff and pork chops served up in modest surroundings. ⓐ Pils iela 9, Sigulda ⓣ 67 97 37 21 ⓛ 08.00–22.00

AFTER DARK

Admirāļu Klubs Dark, dodgy and filled with gamblers. The major attraction is the slots, but you'll also find four pool tables, two snooker tables and air hockey and football. Everything for a guy's night out. ⓐ Pils iela 12, Sigulda ⓣ 26 65 57 47 ⓛ 10.00–22.00 Mon–Thur, 10.00–04.00 Fri & Sat

Aparjods Modelled on a traditional farmstead and decorated with antique clocks and bric-a-brac, this is the best place to have dinner in Sigulda. Ask for a table near the wood-burning fireplace and be prepared to try a menu that carries everything from stuffed pheasant to lobster. ⓐ Ventas iela 1a, Sigulda ⓣ 67 97 22 30 ⓦ www.aparjods.lv ⓛ 12.00–24.00

Melnais Kaķis A smaller cousin to the one in Riga, this establishment caters to all your tastes – a wide menu selection, pool table and slot machines in the back. A good way to while away an evening in the countryside. ⓐ Pils iela 8, Sigulda ⓣ 28 82 20 11

ACCOMMODATION

Aparjods ££ An enthusiastic mix of rural and rustic Latvian influences seamlessly combined with modern conveniences such as satellite TV and whirlpools. In addition to 34 stylishly decorated rooms, an upmarket restaurant and nightclub are also available.
ⓐ Ventas iela 1b, Sigulda
ⓣ 67 97 22 30 Ⓦ www.aparjods.lv

⏷ *The farmstead restaurant of Aparjods*

Līvkalns ££ Just outside the town centre you'll find this quiet hotel complex. The main building is made of wood and even has a traditional reed roof. Located on the shore of a tranquil pond, it also provides a sauna, an excellent restaurant and a banquet hall for weddings.
ⓐ Pēteralas iela, Sigulda ⓣ 67 97 09 16 Ⓦ www.livkalns.lv

Sigulda ££ This charming fieldstone building located in the heart of Sigulda has been expanded and now offers 44 rooms with satellite TV, phone, radio and bathrooms en suite. An elegant restaurant is also available. ⓐ Pils iela 6, Sigulda ⓣ 67 97 22 63 Ⓦ www.hotelsigulda.lv

Spa Hotel Ezeri £££ Only a short cab ride from the train station, 'The Lakes' offers unique interior design based on a photograph hanging over the bed in each room. As if the spa centre wasn't relaxing enough, it also offers a huge garden for peaceful strolls.
ⓐ Siguldas pagasts, Ezeri ⓣ 67 97 30 09 Ⓦ www.hotelezeri.lv

CĒSIS

Cēsis draws both local and foreign tourists to this pastoral region, which has remained virtually untouched despite the two world wars. Cēsis was founded in 1207 with the construction of a stone castle by German knights and it served as the headquarters for the Livonian Order until the 16th century. A city sprang up around the castle and grew so prosperous that it became a member of the Hanseatic League. Cēsis also became the only Latvian city apart from Riga that had a mint for coining money, another testament to its prosperity.

Unfortunately Cēsis fell victim to the wars and plagues of the 17th and 18th centuries and only began to recover in the 19th century when it was finally linked by road and rail to Riga. All the sights of the town centre are within a short distance of each other, making for a compact sightseeing experience.

GETTING THERE

Cēsis is a little farther down the same highway and railway line from Riga as Sigulda, so just add an extra half hour to your trip.

SIGHTS & ATTRACTIONS
Cēsu pils (Cēsis Castle)

Latvia's most impressive and best preserved complex of castle ruins and the most popular site in Cēsis. Some of the original castle of 1207 remains. The castle was expanded under the Livonian Order and the Swedes, but destroyed in 1703 by the Russians. An annex added in the 18th century holds the Cēsis Museum of History and Art.
ⓐ Pils laukums 11 ❶ 64 12 26 15 ❸ 10.00–18.00. Admission charge

❿ *Cēsis boasts one of the best preserved castles in Latvia*

Cēsu vēstures un mākslas muzejs (Cēsis Museum of History and Art)
The exhibits trace Latvian history from prehistoric times to the
Latvian War of Liberation. The tower has an extensive view of Cēsis
and its environs. Also known as the New Castle or Jaunā pils, it was
closed for renovations at the time of writing. ⓐ Pils laukums 9
ⓣ 64 12 18 15 ⓛ 10.00–17.00, closed Mon. Admission charge

Svētā Jāņa baznīca (St John's Church)
Built in the late 13th century, this is now largest church in the region,
a testament to the wealth of the citizens in this flourishing area.
It contains the tombs of several masters of the Livonian Order.
ⓐ Lielā Skolas iela 8 ⓣ 64 12 44 48. Admission charge

Uzvaras piemineklis (Cēsis Victory Monument)
The city's pride and joy, this monument is dedicated to those who
fell in the cause of Latvian freedom at the Battle of Cēsis in 1919.
Erected in the 1920s, it was demolished by the Soviets in the 1950s,
but reconstructed in the 1990s. ⓐ Vienības laukums

TAKING A BREAK

Café Popular £ It truly is quite popular. Either there aren't many
places to eat in Cēsis or everyone knows that dozens of pizzas
served in the cosy cellar of the Kolonna Hotel Cēsis are very tasty
indeed. ⓐ Vienības laukums 1, Cēsis ⓣ 64 12 01 22 ⓛ 11.00–23.00
Mon–Sat, 12.00–22.00 Sun

ACCOMMODATION

Kolonna Hotel Cēsis ££ The best hotel in Cēsis, offers 40 well-
appointed rooms with cable TV, wireless internet, phone, writing
desk and private bathrooms. A restaurant and conference hall are

also at your disposal. ⓐ Vienības laukums 1, Cēsis ⓣ 64 12 01 22
ⓦ www.hotelkolonna.com

GAUJA NATIONAL PARK

The Gauja River carves its way through about 40 km (25 miles) of hills
of Devonian sandstone, as it winds its way from Valmiera to Sigulda
and finally to the sea, leaving behind a surrealistic tangle of carved hills
and forest-covered banks. Established in 1973 specifically to protect
the indigenous flora and fauna, this park is simply the most beautiful
in all of Latvia. Scattered through it are nature trails for hiking, sites
to view various animals and viewing areas with steps and platforms
from which you can see the area's ancient monuments and vistas.

The river is excellent for canoeing, a good way to see the local
scenery. It is possible to rent canoes and rowing boats, guided or
unguided, in Sigulda, Cēsis and Valmiera.

Āraišu ezerpils (Āraiši lake fortress)
The remains of a 9th-century wooden fortified Letgallian town have
been restored to the delight of all. Located on Lake Āraiši on the main
road before Cēsis, it's definitely worth a visit. ⓐ Drabešu pagasts,
Āraišu ezers ⓣ 64 19 72 88 ⓛ 10.00–18.00

Krimuldas baznīca (Krimulda Church)
The oldest church in Latvia still in existence, this ancient architectural
treasure was built in 1205 after the Liv chieftain Kaupo returned from
Rome with the blessings and many gifts, of the reigning pope. Nearby is a
historic building where Lutheran pastors have lived since the 1840s and a
nature trail that supposedly leads to Kaupo's grave. ⓐ Krimuldas pagasts,
Ragana, 'Mācītāja māja' ⓣ 67 70 03 79 ⓦ www.krimuldasbaznica.lv

Līgatnes dabas takas (Līgatne nature trails)

Nature lovers shouldn't pass up an opportunity to take advantage of 5.5 km (1/2 mile) of nature trails that afford hikers excellent views of natural wonders as well as many local animals from unique birds to foxes. ⓐ Līgatnes pagasts ❶ 64 15 33 13 ⓛ 09.00–18.00. Admission charge

Lielstraupes pils (Lielstraupe Castle)

This castle was originally built in the Romanesque style of the 13th century. From the inner courtyard of cobblestones you can view all of the buildings and the gateway leading to the church and the park. Today it houses a drug and alcohol rehabilitation centre. ⓐ Straupes pagasts ❶ 29 42 67 05

Svētā Sīmaņa baznīca (St Simon's Church)

Originally built in 1283, this charming church offers 16th-century tombs, and organ from 1868 and a spire from which you can view the rest of the town. ⓐ Bruņinieku iela 2, Valmiera ❶ 64 20 03 33 ⓦ www.simanis.baznica.lv

Ungurmuiža (Ungurmuiža Manor)

This unique example of 18th-century baroque wooden architecture is open to visitors. Stroll the grounds, take a break in the teahouse and admire the well-preserved murals on the interior walls. ⓐ Raiskuma pagasts ❶ 64 15 82 23 ⓦ www.ungurmuiza.et.lv

Valmieras pilsdrupas (Valmiera castle ruins)

Built in the 13th century as yet another fortification for the Livonian Order, the castle must have been quite a sight in its heyday. Like most castles in Latvia, it was destroyed during the Great Northern War in 1702. You can't miss the towering wall in the centre of the town of Valmiera.

Zvārtes iezis (Zvārte Rock)

One of the most picturesque Devonian rock formations in the region. So good, you won't even mind the small admission charge. ❸ Left bank of the River Amata ☎ 29 33 54 46

OTHER SIGHTS: VIDZEME

Emīla Dārziņa muzejs – Jāņaskola (Emīls Dārziņš's Museum – Jāņaskola)

Emīls Dārziņš's museum tells the story of the composer's life and works. It is an excellent opportunity to listen to *The Melancholy Waltz* and other pieces by a composer who deserves to be better known outside his native country. ❸ Jaunpiebalga pagasts ☎ 64 10 03 51 🕐 10.00–17.00, closed Mon. Admission charge

Kārļa Skalbes Muzejs – Saulrieti (Kārlis Skalbe Museum – Saulrieti)

This is the memorial museum of Kārlis Skalbe, Latvia's answer to Hans Christian Andersen. The house tucks into the landscape and the balcony affords a view of Lake Alauksts. ❸ Vecpiebalga pagasts, 'Saulrieti' ☎ 64 16 42 52 🕐 10.00–17.00, closed Mon. Admission charge

Raunas pilsdrupas (Rauna Castle ruins)

Begun in 1262 by the order of the local Archbishop, this building was one of his main residences, and he clearly wasn't a man of simple tastes, which is great news for the visitor. ❸ Raunas pagasts

Savvaļas zirgu ganības (Wild Horse Pasture)

This is Europe's most northerly enclosure for wild horses. Nine wild horses have been living in a natural habitat since 2002. You can also rent a small house here. ❸ Jaun-Ieviņas, Raunas pagasts ☎ 29 49 51 46 🌐 www.jaun-ievinas.lv

Jūrmala

Once the seaside playground of Tsarist nobles, by the 1920s this area became the summer getaway for the wealthy Riga city dweller. No expense was spared in creating beautiful summer homes by the sea, and you'll see influences of art nouveau, romanticism and classical architecture. What makes this art nouveau area different from that of Riga's? Here the construction was done in wood. The list of architectural monuments has over 400 entries!

Shortly after the end of World War II, Jūrmala became the preferred choice of Soviet citizens to take their holiday. Today the beaches and pine forests are simply teeming with people on weekends, holidays or any day that the sun shines. The long stretches of beach and sand dunes interspersed with fragrant stands of pine make a delightful location to while away a day or two. Jūrmala is the combined name for the string of small towns and resorts that stretch almost 20 km

(12 1/2 miles) along the coast west of Riga, most of which are readily reached by train. Although you can get off the train at every stop and simply head for the beach, most of the action is centred around the towns of Majori, Dzintari and Bulduri. In all there are roughly 15 villages that comprise 'Jūrmala' and in 1959 they were united, mostly for administrative purposes.

At one time the beaches of the Baltic were so polluted you had to be extremely careful about swimming. However, those at Majori and Bulduri have been awarded the coveted 'Blue Flag' that ensures water quality, environmental management, safety and a very important criterion – toilet facilities.

Aside from beach activities you'll find plenty to do at Latvia's seaside. Walking the beaches, dunes and forests is reason enough to visit. And the nightlife is plentiful with restaurants, nightclubs and casinos.

◆ *One of Jūrmala's best beaches is at Majori*

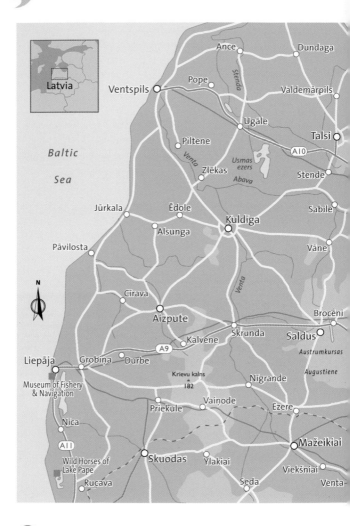

Jūrmala & Western Latvia

0   50 km
0   25 miles

Roja
Upesgrīva
Mērsrags
Vidriži
Ebgures ezers
Saulkrasti
Gulf of Riga
Engure
A1
Carnikava
Vangaži
Ādaži
A2
Kandava
Jūrmala
RIGA
Tukums
Riga International
Zemīte
A10
Salaspils
Abava
Slampe
A6
Olaine
Ķekava
Ogre
LATVIA
A9
Jaunpils
Kalnciems
Misa
Baldone
Jelgava
A7
Dobele
Iecava
Vecumnieki
A8
Stalģene
Iecava
Auce
Kroņauce
Bēne
Lielupe
Mežotne Manor
Eleja
Rundāle
Bauska
Rundāle Palace
N Akmenē
Kamarde
Joniškis
LITHUANIA

○	City
○	Large Town
∩	Small Town
■	POI
—	Main Road
—	Minor Road
✈	Airport
—	Railway

Jūrmala Tourism Information Centre ⓐ Majori, Lienes iela 5
ⓣ 67 14 79 00 ⓦ www.doms.lv ⓛ 09.00–19.00 Mon–Fri,
10.00–17.00 Sat, 10.00–15.00 Sun

GETTING THERE

Trains to Jūrmala depart frequently during the summer from Riga's
Central Station. Expect the trip to the main town of Majori to take
about 35 minutes and to cost roughly 1.50Ls for a return ticket. If you
prefer to do the journey by car (it's 15 km, or nine miles), the drive will
take about half an hour, and you'll soon discover that the road to Jūrmala
is one of the best stretches of highway in the entire country. Please
note, though, that you have to pay a 1Ls toll to enter the town centre.

Easily the most pleasant of all the ways of getting to Jūrmala
is by water, though unfortunately this is only a possibility during
summer weekends, when a few Daugava riverboats make the trip.
It takes about 1 1/2 hours and costs roughly 5Ls one-way. The boats
depart from 11 novembra krastmala and arrive in Majori, just next
to the train station.

SIGHTS & ATTRACTIONS

The primary reason to pry yourself away from the city is to be in the
great outdoors. Yes, there are a few museums and even a concert
hall, but kick off your shoes, slap on some sunscreen and be at one
with the sea.

Dubultu luterāņu baznīca (Dubulti Lutheran Church)
This beautiful church was constructed during the time of the art
nouveau rage in 1909. Like most Lutheran churches, the interior

is simple, but the fantastic spire is very impressive. ❸ Dubulti, Baznīcas iela 13

Jūrmalas brīvdabas muzejs (Jūrmala Open-air Museum)
Created to portray the life of Latvian fishermen in the late 19th and early 20th centuries, this collection is filled with wooden homes, anchors, nets, ropes and antique boats. Located not far from where the Lielupe River flows into the Gulf of Riga, a little way out of town. ❸ Lielupe, Tīklu iela 1a ❶ 67 75 49 09 ❷ 10.00–18.00, closed Mon. Admission charge

Jūrmalas pilsētas muzejs (Jūrmala City Museum)
Much money has been invested into this modern building not far from the Majori train station. Although a small collection of exhibits is available for your perusal, the periodic art and photography exhibitions may be of more interest. ❸ Majori, Tirgoņu iela 29 ❶ 67 76 47 46 ❷ 10.00–17.00, closed Mon & Tues. Admission charge

Seno spēkratu izstāde (Antique Car Exhibition)
Spend an afternoon in this exhibition of classic cars. Lincolns, Mercedes and BMWs are all garaged together, along with some motorcycles (some with sidecars) from days gone by. ❸ Dzintari, Turaidas iela 11 ❶ 29 26 33 29 ❷ 11.00–18.00 May–Sept. Donation requested

CULTURE

Dzintaru koncertzāle (Dzintari Concert Hall) Built in 1936, this sumptuous concert hall is a very popular place for concerts, both indoors and outside in the gardens. ❸ Dzintari, Turaidas iela 1 ❶ 67 76 20 86 ❿ www.dzk.lv

LATVIA'S TRADITIONAL SPA TOWN

Jūrmala owes its very existence to its prime location on the seashore a short distance from Riga. But even before sunbathing became fashionable at the end of the 19th century, aristocrats and wealthy merchants flocked to the area for the reputed healing powers of its local mud and seawater. In 1838, by order of Tsar Nicholas I of Russia, the first genuine spa resort was built in what is now Ķemeri. Bad Kemmern as it was known became a fashionable place for the rich and powerful to relax in the bosom of nature, yet with all of the conveniences the highborn would expect. With the creation of direct rail links to other major population centres, Jūrmala thrived. The early 20th century and years of the first Latvian Republic saw a major construction boom and many of those beautiful wooden cottages are still visible today. During the communist era, Jūrmala became the playground of millions of holidaymakers from around the Soviet Union and to this day it still holds a special place in the hearts of many Russians. So take advantage of all that Jūrmala has to offer and have a massage, take a seawater bath, let steam work its magic on your body in the sauna or let a professional give you a facial with local mud.

RETAIL THERAPY

Like all good beach destinations, this is not where you come to do any serious shopping. The main shops can be found on Jomas iela, and the stretch between Dubulti and Dzintari has the best selection.

Elsewhere it's mostly buckets and spades, floating devices, cheap beach towels and postcards.

TAKING A BREAK/AFTER DARK

Double Coffee £ Great coffee, tasty desserts, breakfast food and even sushi can all be enjoyed here, as well as cocktails. ⓐ Majori, Jomas iela 65/67 ❶ 67 76 31 50 ⓦ www.doublecoffee.lv ❷ 09.00 23.00

Vienos Vārtos £ Jūrmala's only sports bar offers tasty Tērvetes beer on draught, a huge mural of a packed stadium and sports on two TVs. If, however, there are no games to be watched, take advantage of its summer terrace. ⓐ Majori, Jomas iela 61 ❶ 77 76 44 40 ❷ 11.00–24.00

Orients – Jūra £–££ This huge seafood restaurant has elevated its kitschy nautical theme to new heights. Staff dressed in Russian navy shirts bring a variety of fish and meat dishes to your table, or you can skip the middleman and hit the buffet. ⓐ Dzintari, Dzintaru prospekts 2 ❶ 77 76 14 24 ⓦ www.restoran-orient.lv ❷ 12.00–24.00

Seaside ££ Located on the top floor of Hotel Jūrmala Spa, this trendy cocktail bar offers excellent views, a variety of drinks and even a sushi menu. ⓐ Majori, Jomas iela 47/49 ❶ 77 78 44 20 ⓦ www.hoteljurmala.com ❷ 12.00–24.00

Slāvu restorāns ££ With plenty of space on two floors, a huge summer terrace and a menu that caters to the town's single largest ethnic group, Russians, the Slavic Restaurant is never short of diners. Sample a shot of flavoured vodka or order a plate of meat dumplings. ⓐ Majori, Jomas iela 57 ❶ 67 76 14 01 ⓦ www.slavu.lv ❷ 12.00–23.00

Sue's Asia ££ This cosy restaurant has an extensive menu of Indian and Thai cuisine that won't disappoint. The summer terrace on Jomas iela is another reason to give it a try. ⓐ Majori, Jomas iela 74 ⓣ 67 75 59 00 ⓛ 12.00–23.00

Aquarius £££ If you're looking for fusion or nouvelle cuisine and a trendy atmosphere with cutting-edge design this is the place. Located in a modern glass building only a stone's throw from the sea, you won't find a better place for fine dining. ⓐ Bulduri, Bulduru prospekts 33 ⓣ 67 75 10 71 ⓛ 12.00–23.00

Il Sole £££ Even if you're not in the mood for expensive upmarket Italian cuisine, you can still order a drinkette and sit on its fantastic summer terrace overlooking the beach. ⓐ Majori, Jūras iela 23/25 ⓣ 77 77 14 00 ⓛ 12.00–23.00

ACCOMMODATION

Rakstnieku nams £–££ 'The Writers' House' was created as a place where budding novelists and poets could put their thoughts on paper without the distractions of the modern world. Each of the 11 rooms in this charming house not far from the sea is sparsely decorated and meant for people who want to save money and don't need a TV. ⓐ Dubulti, Akas iela 4 ⓣ 77 76 99 65

Amber Sea Hotel ££ Unlike other hotels in the area, this one is built off the main road in a pine forest, yet it's still only a short walk from the beach. Rooms are spacious and tastefully decorated and the suites on the upper floor have luxuriously expansive terraces. ⓐ Dzintari, Dzintaru prospekts 68 ⓣ 67 75 12 97 ⓦ www.amberhotel.lv

Concordia ££ Although the garish pastel colours are little harsh at times, its otherwise spacious and comfortable rooms are incredible value for money. Satellite TV, kitchenettes, balconies and private bathrooms all come as standard. ⓐ Majori, Konkordijas iela 64 ⓣ 29 48 80 81 ⓦ www.concordia.lv

Baltic Beach Hotel ££–£££ Although most of this huge hotel has been renovated to Western standards, the frugal can reserve rooms in the C wing that haven't been upgraded and are therefore much cheaper. A huge spa, two restaurants and three bars are also available as well as a conference centre and excellent views of the sea. ⓐ Majori, Jūras iela 23/25 ⓣ 67 77 14 00 ⓦ www.balticbeach.lv

Lielupe ££–£££ For whatever reason, the owners of this huge skyscraper decided to renovate only half of its 200 rooms, so if you don't mind Soviet-style furnishings you can save loads of money here. Alternatively, you could splurge on the business-class rooms that include satellite TV, mini-bar, phone, safe and even balconies with views. A restaurant, bar, swimming pool and tennis courts are also available. ⓐ Bulduri, Bulduru prospekts 64/68 ⓣ 67 75 27 55 ⓦ www.lielupe.lv

Hotel Jūrmala Spa £££–£££+ This is without a doubt, the best hotel in Jūrmala. The spa centre is immense with a variety of different swimming pools, saunas, over 20 massage rooms and specially designed therapeutic spaces such as a room completely covered in salt to cure sinusitis. An upmarket restaurant, 11th-floor bar, a casino and stylish rooms with modern conveniences such as wireless internet are all at your disposal. ⓐ Majori, Jomas iela 47/49 ⓣ 67 78 44 00 ⓦ www.hoteljurmala.com

Western Latvia

Do you fancy a day trip to long sandy beaches or scenic forest bogs? Maybe some time spent viewing the lavish excesses of some 18th-century dukes? Many of Western Latvia's tourist attractions are within an easy day trip of Riga.

Begin with a trip to the Zemgale region, an area that extends south of Riga to the Lithuanian border. Although the landscape is largely flat and somewhat uninteresting, it is decorated with two sumptuous palaces – the neo-classical Mežotne Manor and the baroque Rundāle Palace. Both architectural monuments are within easy reach of Bauska, which boasts an impressive medieval castle, and all three places can be visited in a single day.

Kurzeme is home to some of Latvia's most spectacular natural scenery. The coast road west from Riga is a ribbon that runs along an unspoiled coast to where the Baltic Sea meets the Gulf of Riga. This area is filled with intriguing towns waiting to be explored and spectacular and varied landscapes.

Kuldīga, filled with medieval atmosphere and charm, has existed since at least the 9th century, but it was not until the German invaders of the 13th century arrived that a castle and other significant buildings were established. Over the centuries the town grew, and today the town's pride is the preserved architecture and bridge constructions. The Old Town Hall and Town Square, built in the 17th century, are the centrepiece of the town. Kuldīga also has one of Latvia's most beautiful natural wonders, Europe's widest waterfall, Ventas Rumba.

Liepāja is possibly the furthest you will travel in Latvia while using Riga as your base. This is a city that embraces its maritime traditions.

▶ *Liepāja is considered to be the cradle of Latvian rock music*

The lighthouses of Liepāja were most likely the first ones to welcome European sailors, as people have lived in this area for more than 750 years. At one time the city was the capital of Latvia, and it has a unique heritage of being governed by Swedish kings, German barons and Russian tsars.

A visit to the seashore, or *jūrmala*, of the Liepāja region is a real surprise. Thanks to the presence of the Soviet Navy for almost 50 years, this area has remained largely untouched. Take some time to wander the empty beaches backed by juniper and pine trees. You can also explore abandoned tsarist forts that are slowly receding into the sea.

SIGHTS & ATTRACTIONS

Bauska Castle ruins
Built by the Livonian Order at the confluence of the Mūsa and Mēmele rivers in the 15th century, this magnificent castle is currently being restored, but is open to the public. Explore the castle grounds and don't forget to climb up to the observation tower for great views.
ⓐ Pilskalns, Bauska ❶ 63 92 37 93 Ⓦ www.tourism.bauska.lv
🕙 09.00–19.00. Admission charge

Karosta (Russian Naval Port)
No trip to Liepāja is complete with a trip to the nearly abandoned naval port that has been used by the Russian Empire, the Latvian army and the Soviet navy. Visit a colossal Orthodox church surrounded by dilapidated communist housing estates, ruined tsarist-era forts falling into the sea and take a tour of the Karosta prison, which is rumoured to be haunted. ⓐ Karosta, Liepāja Ⓦ www.karosta.lv, www.karostascietums.lv

Kuldīgas vecpilsēta (Kuldīga Old Town)

Wander the maze of medieval streets that comprise Kuldīga's old town and see medieval churches, charming 17th-century wooden buildings with red-tiled roofs and the picturesque Alekšupīte river that traverses the city. Europe's widest waterfall is another major attraction.

Mežotnes pils (Mežotne Manor)

Construction of this neo-classical manor was completed in 1802. Since then it has been used and abused by aristocracy, schools and invading armies, but today it has been completely restored and now serves as an elegant upmarket hotel. ⓐ Mežotnes pils, Bauskas rajons ① 63 96 07 11 Ⓦ www.mezotnespils.lv Admission charge

Rundāles pils (Rundāle Palace)

Make sure you find time on your schedule to visit this beautiful Baroque palace. It was the brainchild of Italian architect, Francesco Bartolomeo Rastrelli, the designer of St Petersburg's Winter Palace. The building took more than 28 years to build and decorate. This palace was once part of the fortune of the Duke of Courland. ⓐ Pilsrundāle, Bauskas rajons ① 63 96 22 74 Ⓦ www.rundale.net ① 10.00–17.00. Admission charge

Svētā Trīsvienības luterāņu baznīca (Holy Trinity Church)

The crumbling white façade could use a bit of spackle and paint, but the impressive rococo interior is guaranteed to make your jaw drop. Even more amazing is its enormous pipe organ that was the world's largest when it was first played. For a small fee the caretaker will take you up the creaking wooden stairs to the observation platform. ⓐ Lielā iela 9, Liepāja ① 63 42 22 08 ① 10.00–18.00

Ventspils pils (Ventspils Castle)

Built at the tail end of the 13th century, this castle is unlike any other castle in Latvia because it has generally retained its original shape and design. It also houses the Ventspils Museum. ⓐ Jāņa iela 17, Ventspils ① 63 62 20 31 ⓦ www.ventspilsmuzejs.lv ④ 10.00–17.00. Admission charge

CULTURE

Aušanas darbnīca (Weavers' Workshop)

Watch local weavers create blankets and clothing on antique looms in an historic 17th-century building where King Charles XII once stayed during the Great Northern War. You can also buy local crafts here. ⓐ Kungu iela 26, Liepāja ① 63 42 32 86 ④ 09.00–17.00, closed Sat & Sun

Kino Balle (Balle Cinema)

Anything from popular European films to Hollywood blockbusters shown in their original languages with Latvian and Russian subtitles. ⓐ Rožu laukums 5/6, Liepāja ① 63 48 06 38 ⓦ www.kinoballe.lv

Liepājas teātris (Liepāja Theatre)

The oldest professional theatre in all Latvia, founded in 1917, performs mostly musicals for both adults and children. ⓐ Teātra iela 4, Liepāja ① 63 42 21 21 ⓦ www.liepajasteatris.lv

Liepājas simfoniskais orķestris (Liepāja Symphony Orchestra)

Liepāja's symphony orchestra is one of the oldest in the Baltic States. It frequently debuts new music by Latvian composers. ⓐ Graudu iela 50, Liepāja ① 63 42 55 88 ⓦ www.orkestris-liepaja.lv

Rio Ventspils' only cinema could be an option on a rainy day.
ⓐ Pils iela 28, Ventspils ① 63 62 46 97

RETAIL THERAPY

Pētertirgus (Peter's Market)
Although the main building was erected in 1910, hundreds of smaller stalls spill out onto the market square where you can buy anything from flowers and crafts to fresh produce. ⓐ Kuršu iela 5/7/9, Liepāja ① 63 42 35 17 Ⓦ www.petertirgus.lv ⓛ 08.00–18.00 Mon–Sat, 08.00–14.00 Sun

TAKING A BREAK

Fontaine Deli Snack £ Delicious, inexpensive burgers, a wide variety of pizzas, nachos and burritos as well as Asian stir fries can all be had here 24 hours a day. It also delivers. ⓐ Dzirnavu iela 4, Liepāja ① 63 48 85 23 Ⓦ www.fontainepalace.lv

Pastnieka māja £–££ 'The Postman's House' may be the only restaurant in Eastern Europe with a postal theme. The extensive menu of Latvian and international dishes is presented in an envelope, the interior is eclectic and the service is excellent. ⓐ Fr. Brīvzemnieka iela 53, Liepāja ① 63 40 75 21 Ⓦ www.pastniekamaja.lv ⓛ 11.00–24.00

Melnais sivēns ££ 'The Black Piglet' is located in Ventspils Castle and, not surprisingly, offers its patrons a medieval theme complete with waiting staff in period costume, massive wooden furniture and authentic flatware. In the summer you can also take advantage of

● Dine to a postal theme at Pastnieka māja

its more modern terrace with views of the port. ⓐ Jāņa iela 17, Ventspils ❶ 63 62 23 96 ◷ 11.00–23.00

Zutis ££ 'The Eel' is owned and operated by two bohemian sisters from Riga. Their goal was to open a casual restaurant and bar with excellent service and refined cuisine. They succeeded. ⓐ Ed. Veidenbauma iela 8, Liepāja ❶ 63 48 11 13 ◷ 12.00–24.00

AFTER DARK

Fontaine Palace The best rock club in Latvia is located in a renovated 19th-century warehouse on the harbour canal. Owned by a Dane who fell in love with Liepāja, its stage is almost always occupied by foreign and local acts from Finnish metal bands to Latvian punks. ⓐ Dzirnavu iela 4, Liepāja ⓣ 63 48 85 10 ⓦ www.fontainepalace.lv ⓛ 24 hours

Grilbārs Bruno This cosy bar in the cellar of the Amrita Hotel offers a good selection of Latvian draught beers, a great menu of pub food from fish and chips to breakfast food and even some bar games like *novus* – a Latvian billiard game of sorts. ⓐ Rīgas iela 7/9, Liepāja ⓣ 63 40 34 34 ⓛ 17.00–01.00 Tues–Thur, 15.00–01.00 Fri & Sat, 15.00–23.00 Sun

Latvia's 1st Rock Café One of Latvia's largest bars and nightclubs occupies four floors of a building on a central square including a rooftop terrace and a cellar bar. Listen to live acts at night, play pool, order inexpensive food or hit the dance floor. ⓐ Stendera iela 18/20, Liepāja ⓣ 63 48 15 55 ⓦ www.pablo.lv ⓛ 09.00–06.00

ACCOMMODATION

Fontaine Hotel ££ This charming building is over 100 years old, yet its one of Latvia's best boutique hotels. A curio shop serves as a reception area, Soviet army footlockers are used as coffee tables and all rooms include DVD players. Affordable and unpretentious, you absolutely must book in advance. ⓐ Jūras iela 24, Liepāja ⓣ 63 42 09 56 ⓦ www.fontaine.lv

Fontaine Royal ££ This sprawling brick warehouse at the harbour has been completely renovated and now offers inexpensive rooms with unique interior design and all of the modern conveniences one would expect. A huge restaurant and a spa centre are also available.
ⓐ Stūrmaņu iela 1, Liepāja ⓣ 63 48 97 77 ⓦ www.fontaine.lv

Libava £££ A converted 18th-century customs house on the harbour canal has been transformed into one of the city's best design hotels. Eat breakfast in the palm garden atrium or dine on excellent, yet affordable, nouvelle cuisine at its cellar restaurant.
ⓐ Vecā Ostmala 29, Liepāja ⓣ 63 42 45 43 ⓦ www.libava.lv

Promenade Hotel £££–£££+ For luxury and location you can't beat this converted 19th-century warehouse. All rooms include unique designer interiors, some with balconies, and spectacular views of the yacht marina below. An upmarket restaurant is also available.
ⓐ Vecā Ostmala 40, Liepāja ⓣ 63 48 82 88 ⓦ www.promenadehotel.lv

● *A passenger train glides over Riga's railway bridge*

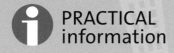

PRACTICAL
information

Directory

GETTING THERE
By air
The easiest way to get to Riga is to fly. Riga International Airport is fully modern and highly rated among European airports. It is served by direct flights from dozens of cities in Europe, Asia and America. Riga is served by daily flights from most major cities in Europe. Low-cost air services from the UK to Riga are offered by:

AirBaltic Ⓦ www.airbaltic.lv
Ryanair Ⓦ www.ryanair.com

Many people are aware that air travel emits CO_2, which contributes to climate change. You may be interested in the possibility of lessening the environmental impact of your flight through Climate Care, which offsets your CO_2 by funding environmental projects around the world. Visit Ⓦ www.climatecare.org

By rail
There is a direct service from Vilnius, Minsk, Moscow and St. Petersburg. Services are available from the rest of Europe via Kaunas or Vilnius. The train service in Latvia is among the worst in Europe, as it has not been properly maintained or upgraded in recent years. Eurail passes are not valid in Latvia. The monthly *Thomas Cook European Rail Timetable* has up-to-date schedules for European international and Latvian train services.

Riga Central Railway Station is located just outside the southeast end of the Old Town at Stacijas laukums. It has been recently renovated, and has a currency exchange, ATM, shops, a post office, ticket booths, restaurants and news-stands. Unless you have heavy luggage it is easier to leave on foot, as many of the major hotels are within a 10-minute walk, but several dodgy taxis can be flagged down just outside the station. Always agree on a price before leaving. A taxi to anywhere in the Old Town or City Centre should not cost more than 3 to 5 Ls.

Thomas Cook European Rail Timetable 🛈 (UK) 01733 416477; (USA) 1 800 322 3834 🅦 www.thomascookpublishing.com

By road

Driving from the UK can take a long time, the total distance from Calais being about 2160 km (1342 miles). The roads are good and fast through Western Europe, but once you reach Poland the pace will slow, as there are few multilane fast highways in Poland and the Baltic states.

If you want someone else to do the driving, bus is preferable to train. The main long-distance bus terminal is located at the southeast end of the Old Town, just one block away from the railway station. There is a regular service from Tallinn and Vilnius, with connections to most other major European cities. The bus terminal has a currency exchange, ATMs, news-stands, a pharmacy, and a restaurant.

Taxis can be flagged down just outside the terminal, but they are unreliable at best. If you must take a cab call one of the companies listed in the Taxis section on page 58. Old Riga is only a five-minute walk away.

By water

The ferry terminal is located about 1 km northwest of the Old Town. There are ferry connections from Stockholm by Tallink and from Lubeck, Germany by Baltic Ferries. The ferry terminal has a currency exchange, an ATM and a restaurant. Trams 5, 7 and 9 leave from in front of the

● *Many tourists arrive at Riga's ferry terminal*

terminal, and will take you to the Old Town and to the City Centre.
The cost is only 0.30Ls, and tickets can be purchased directly from
the driver. Taxis are available just outside the terminal entrance.
A ride to the Old Town or city centre should take about ten minutes,
and cost about 5Ls.

Baltic Ferries Ⓦ www.balticferries.nl
Scandlines Ⓦ www.scandlines.lv
Tallink Ⓦ www.tallink.lv

ENTRY FORMALITIES
Documentation
A valid passport is required to enter the country. Since Latvia joined
the EU in 2004, entry into the country has become very easy for most
people. Entry from another EU country is normally very quick, although
entry from Russia can take some time. Citizens of Canada, Australia,
New Zealand and the USA, and of EU-member states, do not require

a visa unless they plan to stay longer than 90 days. Citizens of most other countries, including South Africa, will require a visa, available on entry at Riga airport but not at land borders.

Customs
The importation of guns, narcotics, pornography and other normally banned material is forbidden. There are no restrictions on the amount of hard currency you can bring in or take out. Exporting items from Latvia is easy unless the object dates from before 1945, in which case the item is taxed and also requires an export permit issued by the Ministry of Culture (ⓐ Valdemāra iela 11a ⓦ www.km.gov.lv).

MONEY
The national currency is the Latvian Lat. The Lat is broken down into 100 santīmi. There are coins of 1, 2, 5, 10, 20, and 50 santīmi, and of 1 and 2 Lats. There are banknotes of 5, 10, 20, 50, 100 and 500 Lats.

Traveller's cheques and Eurocheques can be exchanged in banks. Note that foreign banknotes that are torn, marked with ink, or very old are only accepted at considerable discount, or not at all.

Nearly all hotels, shops and restaurants accept Visa and MasterCard while Diner's Club and American Express are seldom accepted anywhere in Latvia.

Banks and ATMs are plentiful and easy to find in Riga. All banks offer currency exchange. Exchange offices are also found in larger hotels, the airport, railway station, passenger port, major shopping centres and throughout the Old Town.

HEALTH, SAFETY & CRIME
Latvia is relatively low-risk in terms of health problems. No immunisations are required before visiting, although if you plan to hike in wooded or

boggy areas you should be vaccinated against tick-borne encephalitis. This presents itself as a rash, possibly with flu-like symptoms, and left untreated it can have long-term effects and possibly even result in death. If you have any reason to think that you have contracted it from a tick, seek immediate treatment. To protect yourself, cover up legs and arms when walking in long grass and if a tick does attach itself to you remove it at once.

The tap water is safe to drink, although it is frequently less than palatable.

Minor ailments can usually be treated at pharmacies (*aptiekas*), which carry a wide range of international drugs from painkillers to antibiotics. Major complaints are best treated at a hospital (*slimnīca*). Emergency treatment is very cheap but if you are admitted to hospital you will naturally be charged a larger fee for care.

The standard of medical care is high, and not a cause for concern. Most doctors speak English, but other health care workers may not. There are private clinics with English-speaking doctors in Riga – see Emergencies on page 154 for details. EU reciprocal health care privileges apply in Latvia: UK residents should obtain a European Health Insurance Card (EHIC) before travelling. However, it is still wise (and for visitors from outside the EU, absolutely essential) to take out comprehensive travel insurance with good health cover.

Latvia has a relatively low crime rate. However, tourist attractions, such as Old Town, are prime hunting grounds for sneak thieves, muggers and pickpockets. Try to keep mobile phones and camera equipment out of sight as much as possible, and leave expensive jewellery at home. If you have a car, be sure to park it in a guarded and well-lit lot, as car theft is common. Unfortunately, there have been reports of racist attacks on dark-skinned visitors by Russian skinheads, even in broad daylight. Be vigilant and avoid groups of inebriated youths who look like they have nothing to do.

If you are the victim of crime, be patient with the police. Many officers, especially the older ones, are not fluent in English. The police are generally courteous and businesslike, but can be slow in filling out crime report forms. They are generally unsympathetic to foreign drivers who break traffic regulations and will insist on applying on-the-spot fines. Make a copy of your passport and other important travel documents such as air tickets. If these items are lost, replacement will be much easier with these copies at hand.

Visitors are required to carry identification at all times, although it is unlikely that you will be required to produce it except when entering and leaving the country.

If you need a policeman, look for a man in blue

△ *The Laima clock will help you keep track of local opening hours*

OPENING HOURS

You'll find the majority of business establishments are open from 09.00 to 17.00. Lunch is the main meal of the day in Latvia, so expect restaurants and eateries to be quite busy between 13.00 and 15.00. Banks are normally open from 09.00 to 18.00 on weekdays, while some are also open on Saturday from 10.00 to 15.00. Shops generally stay open until 18.00, some later on Thursday and Friday evenings, keeping limited hours on Saturday and closing completely on Sunday. The exceptions are supermarkets and shopping centres that are usually open daily from 10.00 to 22.00.

TOILETS

Brush up on the correct symbols to avoid embarrassment. Men's facilities are designated by a V, a K, or a triangle pointing downward. Women should look for an S, a D, or a triangle pointing upward.

A surprisingly clean and tidy exception to the generally poor public toilet situation are the facilities in the newly renovated central train station. Most hotels or restaurants are pretty accommodating about allowing you to use their loos without being a customer.

CHILDREN

Riga may not be the best city to bring young children to visit. Older ones may enjoy parts of the city that look as though they have stepped from their history and storybooks. Finding family-friendly eateries may be a bit of a challenge and the cobble-stoned streets of the Old Town will definitely throw some navigational challenges in the way of your pram. Good places for kids include:

- **Latvian State Puppet Theatre** Puppetry remains a strong art in many parts of Europe and the plays presented here are top notch. Very young children, from ages 2-6, will benefit the most from this type of performance. A nice feature is that the chair height will adjust so that even the smallest child will still have a good view of the stage. ⓐ Barona iela 16/18 ☎ 67 28 53 55 ⓦ www.puppet.lv

- **Lido Recreation Centre** This giant log cabin offers three floors of Latvian food and drink as well as dozens of children's attractions including a skating rink in winter. ⓐ Krasta iela 76 ☎ 67 50 44 20 ⓦ www.ac.lido.lv 🕐 10.00–23.00

- **Līvu Akvaparks** A kiddie pool, wave pools, six water slides and a tubing river will keep children of all ages happy all day long. The largest water park in Latvia even offers a bar for weary parents. ⓐ Viestura iela 36, Lielupe, Jūrmala ☎ 67 75 56 36 ⓦ www.akvaparks.lv 🕐 12.00–22.00 Mon–Fri, 10.00–22.00 Sat & Sun

- **Open-air Ethnographic Museum** Latvian life as it was once upon a time. Farmsteads, fishing villages, windmills and churches have been relocated to this open-air museum to be preserved for posterity. Craftsmen offer daily demonstrations. ⓐ Brīvības gatve 440 ☎ 67 99 45 15 ⓦ www.virmus.lv 🕐 10.00–17.00

● *Children will be enchanted by the many traditional toys and puppets*

- **Riga Circus** The Riga Circus is the only permanent circus in the Baltics. It features some unusual acts including performing pigs and domestic cats that don't always care to perform. But children of all ages always enjoy a circus. ⓐ Merķeļa iela 4 ① 67 21 32 79 ⓦ www.cirks.lv

- **Riga Zoo** Set in a pine-tree forest the Riga Zoo is a remarkably varied zoo with all the standard zoo fare such as bears and some intriguing inclusions like Tibetan wild donkeys and an insect centre. The zoo and the surrounding Forest Park is a favourite strolling area for residents. ⓐ Meža prospekts 1 ① 67 51 84 09 ① 10.00–18.00 ⓦ www.rigazoo.lv

- **T.G.I.Friday's** This American chain provides a kids' menu, colouring books and sometimes balloons. ⓐ Kaļķu iela 6 ① 67 22 90 71 ⓦ www.rrg.lv ① 12.00–24.00

- **Vairāk Saules** A kids' menu and all the Lego a child's heart could desire in a smoke-free environment. ⓐ Dzirnavu iela 60 ⓘ 67 28 28 78 ⓦ www.vairaksaules.lv ⓛ 09.00–23.00

COMMUNICATIONS

Phones

The telephone system in Latvia is reliable and easy to use. All numbers within the country are eight-digit and there are no area codes. Riga has a good supply of public telephone boxes, but they use magnetic cards and not coins. The public phones offer international direct dialling, and many have English language instructions posted inside.

If you will be using a pay phone, you can purchase a Lattelecom card at most kiosks (ⓦ www.lattelecom.lv). These are available in values of 2, 3, and 5Ls. These are available for both national and international calls, and can be purchased at news-stands, post offices and most kiosks.

If you have a GSM mobile phone, it is possible to avoid heavy roaming charges by purchasing a prepaid SIM card from one of the local services, such as O-Karte or Zelta Zivtiņa. Starter packs and refills are available at newspaper kiosks and grocery shops.

Post

The Latvian postal system is quite reliable. The main Riga Post Office is conveniently located at ⓐ Stacijas laukums 2, just southeast of the

CALLING INTO AND OUT OF LATVIA IS EASY

To call in, simply dial your country's international access code, then 371 (Latvia's country code) and then the eight-digit number. To call out, dial 00, then the country code and then the local number (omitting the first 0 in the case of UK area codes).

Old Town, and near both the railway station and bus terminal. Other centrally located post offices include ⓐ Brīvības bulvāris 32 and ⓐ Grēcinieku 1.

Besides handling mail and stamps, the post office can be used to send and receive faxes, and to make international telephone calls. Unfortunately, many Latvians also use the post office to pay their bills so queues can be shockingly long. Take a number and grumble your dissatisfaction with everyone else.

Sending a letter to Europe costs 0.45Ls, and to North America and Australasia costs 0.55Ls. For information on postal services ⓣ 800 8001 ⓦ www.pasts.lv

Internet

Riga and other large cities in Latvia are well served by internet cafés, although in smaller towns they may be difficult to find. Many cafés and hotels also offer wireless internet access for laptop owners. Here are some of the most central internet points in Riga:

DR Centrs Eight computers, beer, wine and other types of alcohol. Cost: 0.90Ls/hour ⓐ Elizabetes iela 75 ⓣ 67 28 25 59 ⓒ 09.30–22.00 Mon–Fri, 10.00–21.00 Sat & Sun

Pasta centrs Sakta The post office runs a top-notch internet café at its most central location. ⓐ Brīvības bulvāris 32 ⓣ 67 50 28 15 ⓦ www.pasts.lv ⓒ 07.00–22.00

Planēta Have to stop mid-sightseeing to check your email? This Old Town location has four rooms of computers. Cost: 0.60Ls/hour. ⓐ Pils iela 14 ⓣ 67 22 66 73 ⓒ 24 hours

MEDIA
Television

Many hotels are equipped with a wide range of cable and satellite channels offering programs in English, German and Russian. Most locals tune in to state-owned channels LTV1 and LTV7 for serious news and culture. Game shows, local dramas, sports and American and German TV series and films dubbed in Latvian are shown on LNT, TV3 and TV5.

Radio

In Riga, you get a wide range of music, from progressive rock to golden oldies to classical:

BBC (100.5 FM) Virtual heaven for World Service fanatics. BBC in English 24 hours a day

Classical Music (103.7 FM)

European Hit Radio (104.3 FM) Mostly techno and European hits

Radio Naba (93.1 FM) Funky, alternative music

SWH Rock (89.2 FM) Classic and modern rock. SWH+ in Russian is at 105.7 FM; music and news

Star FM (106.2 FM) A popular station in Riga. Plays mostly techno

Magazines and newspapers

The English-language magazine *Riga In Your Pocket* (ⓦ www.inyourpocket.com) is available at tourist information offices, hotels, restaurants and the airport, and is a great source of information on entertainment and events and of restaurant reviews. The main newspaper for expatriates is the *Baltic Times*, available at news-stands.

Latvia boasts a wide array of magazines and newspapers for a country of only 2.3 million inhabitants. If your Latvian language skills aren't quite up to speed, don't fret. Major English-language newspapers and magazines are available at Narvesen kiosks in Old Riga and the city centre.

ELECTRICITY

The electrical system in Latvia is very reliable. It is 220 volts AC, 50 hertz. The plug is two pin, European style. Travellers from the UK will need to take adapters with them for their 3-pin appliances; North American visitors will need a transformer. It is easier to purchase these items before setting off than to find a shop selling them in Riga.

TRAVELLERS WITH DISABILITIES

Sadly, Riga has a long way to go to become truly wheelchair-accessible. Tourist offices can be especially helpful in determining if there is suitable accommodation if you make your request in advance. It's a good idea to double-check any information you receive, as some establishments will advertise services that are still to be implemented.

If you travel with a wheelchair have it serviced before your departure and carry any essentials you may need to effect repairs. Associations dealing with your particular disability can be excellent sources of information. The following contacts may be helpful.

Latvia Apeirons ⓐ Valdemāra iela 38 ⓣ 67 29 92 77 ⓦ www.apeirons.lv

United Kingdom & Republic of Ireland
Irish Wheelchair Association ⓐ Blackheath Drive, Clontarf, Dublin 3 ⓣ 01 818 6400 ⓦ www.iwa.ie

USA & Canada
Access-able ⓦ www.access-able.com
Society for Accessible Travel & Hospitality (SATH) ⓐ 347 5th Avenue, New York, NY 10016 ⓣ 212/447-7284 ⓦ www.sath.org

Australia & New Zealand
Australian Council for Rehabilitation of the Disabled (ACROD) ⓐ PO Box 60, Curtin, ACT 2605, Australia ⓣ 02 6282 4333 ⓦ www.acrod.org.au
Disabled Persons Assembly ⓐ 173–5 Victoria Street, Wellington, NZ ⓣ 04 801 9100 ⓦ www.dpa.org.nz

TOURIST INFORMATION

City of Riga Information Centre Very helpful tourist information centre that offers a wide range of information in a variety of languages. Can assist with hotel bookings and other useful services. 🄰 Rātslaukums 6 📞 67 03 79 00 📠 67 03 79 00 🌐 www.rigatourism.com 🕙 10.00–19.00

There are also branches at the central bus station and central railway station:

Bus station 🄰 Prāgas iela 1 📞 67 22 05 55 🕙 09.00–19.00
Railway station 🄰 Stacijas laukums 2 📞 67 23 38 15 🕙 10.00–18.30

Latvian Tourist Information Centre This bureau is very useful if you intend to explore outside the city on one of the out of town trips. It can provide maps and useful advice as well as arrange hotel reservations. 🄰 Smilšu iela 4 📞 67 22 46 64 📠 67 22 46 65 🌐 www.latviatourism.lv 🕙 09.00–18.00.

Useful websites

The following official and unofficial websites are all also good sources of information for planning your trip:
🌐 **www.art.lv** Listings of galleries, with links to artists
🌐 **www.culture.lv** Lots of links to Riga's cultural life
🌐 **www.folklora.lv** The scoop on the Latvian folk scene
🌐 **www.inspirationriga.lv** Official site of Riga Tourism
🌐 **www.inyourpocket.com** Up-to date listings of culture, restaurants and accommodation. Also offers online hotel reservations
🌐 **www.lv** General directory of Latvian resources on the web
🌐 **www.li.lv** The Latvian Institute publishes a wealth of information about Latvia
🌐 **www.virtual.lv** City plans and maps on line
🌐 **www.virtualriga.lv** Topical city and news guide

Emergencies

EMERGENCY NUMBERS
In an emergency call:
Fire 01
Police 02
Ambulance 03
Pan-European Assistance 112. This number will connect you with someone to assist you in English.

Medical emergencies
There is an increase of professional options for general medical treatment. Some Western-trained doctors have set up private practices in Riga, for instance.

EMERGENCY PHRASES

Help!	**Fire!**	**Stop!**
Palīgā!	Deg!	Stāt!
Pa-lee-gaa!	*Deg!*	*Staat!*

Call an ambulance/a doctor/the police/the fire service!
Izsauciet ātro palīdzību/ārstu/ policiju/ugunsdzēsējus!
Iz-sau-tsiet aat-ro pa-lee-dzee-bu/aarstu/ po-lit-see-yu/ u-guns-dzes-eyus!

Hospitals

Hospital Gaiļezers ⓐ Hipokrāta iela 2 ⓣ 67 04 24 24 Ⓦ www.gailes.lv

Pauls Stradiņš Clinical University Hospital ⓐ Pilsoņu iela 13
ⓣ 67 06 96 00 Ⓦ www.stradini.lv

University Children's Hospital ⓐ Vienības gatve 45 ⓣ 67 06 44 99
Ⓦ www.bkus.lv

Doctors

ARS Clinic Has a 24-hour service in English ⓐ Skolas iela 5
ⓣ 720 10 07

DS Medical Centre ⓐ Elizabetes iela 57 ⓣ 67 22 99 42
Ⓦ www.dsmc.lv

Dentists

Elladent ⓐ Vīlandes iela 18 ⓣ 67 33 30 04 Ⓦ www.elladent.lv

Sandent ⓐ Hanzas iela 6 ⓣ 67 33 44 26 Ⓦ www.sandent.lv

Vanags' Dental Clinic ⓐ Cēsu iela 31-k2 ⓣ 67 22 07 35
Ⓦ www.vanagaklinika.lv

EMBASSIES & CONSULATES

Australia (Honorary Consulate) ⓐ Arhitektu iela 1-305 ⓣ 67 22 42 51

Canada ⓐ Baznīcas iela 20/22 ⓣ 67 81 39 45

New Zealand Contact UK Embassy

Republic of Ireland ⓐ Alberta iela 13 ⓣ 67 03 93 70

South Africa Contact UK Embassy

UK ⓐ Alunāna iela 5 ⓣ 67 77 47 00

USA ⓐ Raiņa bulvaris 7 ⓣ 67 03 62 00

INDEX

WHAT'S IN YOUR GUIDEBOOK?

Independent authors Impartial up-to-date information from our travel experts who meticulously source local knowledge.

Experience Thomas Cook's 165 years in the travel industry and guidebook publishing enriches every word with expertise you can trust.

Travel know-how Contributions by thousands of staff around the globe, each one living and breathing travel.

Editors Travel-publishing professionals, pulling everything together to craft a perfect blend of words, pictures, maps and design.

You, the traveller We deliver a practical, no-nonsense approach to information, geared to how you really use it.

Editorial/project management: Lisa Plumridge
Copy editor: Paul Hines
Layout/DTP: Alison Rayner
Proofreader: Yyvonne Bergman

The publishers would like to thank the following individuals and
organisations for supplying their copyright photographs for this
book: A1 Pix, pages 1, 5, 15, 21, 40/41, 68, 81, 83, 90–1, 101, 107, 109,
113, 115, 120–1, & 148; Ann Carroll Burgess & Tom Burgess, pages 7,
19, 24, 72 87, 89 & 142; Latvia Tourism, pages 13, 105 & 145; Stillman
Rogers Photography, page 136; Martins Zaprauskis, pages 17, 20,
23, 29, 31, 37, 44, 47, 59, 63, 77, 99, 131 & 146; Andrejs Zavadskis/
iStockphoto.com, page 139.

Send your thoughts to
books@thomascook.com

- Found a great bar, club, shop or must-see sight that we don't feature?
- Like to tip us off about any information that needs a little updating?
- Want to tell us what you love about this handy little guidebook and
  more importantly how we can make it even handier?

Then here's your chance to tell all! Send us ideas, discoveries and
recommendations today and then look out for your valuable input
in the next edition of this title.

Email the above address (stating the title) or write to:
CitySpots Project Editor, Thomas Cook Publishing, PO Box 227,
Coningsby Road, Peterborough PE3 8SB, UK.